ADVANCE PRAISE FOR

Openness Unhindered

This is a remarkable book—uncommonly wise, unrelentingly gentle, and uncompromisingly biblical. I know few people who can be as heartfelt and as tough minded at the same time. Whether Rosaria is telling her God-driven personal story, calling the church to a renewed emphasis on hospitality, or arguing for the importance of words and definitions, I found this work to be an inspiring mix of humility, honesty, compassion, and courage. I hope it is read far and wide, and read deeply too.

—Kevin DeYoung, Senior Pastor, University Reformed Church

Who am I and how do my deep-seated desires fit into my identity? This is a question of utmost importance for the true follower of Christ. With truth and grace, Dr. Rosaria Butterfield delivers another outstanding book—this time addressing the issues of sexuality and identity.

The release of this book couldn't have come at a more opportune time when the Church is awakening to the need to better minister to people navigating through issues of sexual identity. This is the book. And it is a must read for the theologically astute and gospel-centered person. Whether you agree or disagree, read it. You will be challenged and uplifted, and you will get to know in a small way a woman who loves God with all her heart, soul, mind and strength.

—Christopher Yuan, speaker and author of *Out of a Far Country: A Gay Son's Journey to God*

In an age where Facebook offers over fifty gender options, confusion about identity abounds as people try to discover who they really are. Thankfully, like the seasoned trail guide she is, in *Openness, Unhindered* Rosaria Butterfield offers knowledgeable, compassionate direction to lead people in their search for true identity. As you read this book, you will hear echoes and explanations of the ancient paradox that all true sojourners eventually learn: that to find yourself, you must first lose yourself.

—Barry York, professor of pastoral theology, Reformed Presbyterian Theological Seminary

Who is Rosaria Butterfield? A wife? A mother? A former tenured English Professor? A former lesbian? Yes, all of these. But, fundamentally, and most importantly, she is a child of God, who belongs to Jesus Christ. That is her chief identity; and that identity makes all the difference in the world as she approaches the sensitive and difficult topic of sexual sin.

But—and I believe this is vital—we have a book before us that explains what it means to be a true Christian. And when we understand what it means to be a true Christian, we will quickly realize, as Rosaria Butterfield has, that God's grace for us in Christ is sufficient for all of our various struggles and sins. *Openness Unhindered* is a courageous book, warmly written, theologically rich, and precisely what the church needs right now.

—Mark Jones, author of *Antinomianism* and minister at Faith Vancouver Presbyterian Church of America

Rosaria Butterfield is a gift from God to the church. She brings together so many rare combinations: courage and compassion, provocation and wisdom, profundity and accessibility. Virtually every page of this new book overflows with insights on sexual identity, our disordered rebellion, and what it means to commune with the Triune God to whom we are united. Taken to heart, this book will change not only conversations but the very way we live before God.

—Justin Taylor, co-editor for John Owen's *Overcoming Sin and Temptation*

Openness Unhindered

Openness Unhindered

Further Thoughts of an Unlikely Convert on
Sexual Identity and Union with Christ

Rosaria Champagne Butterfield

Crown & Covenant
PUBLICATIONS

Pittsburgh, Pennsylvania

© 2015 Rosaria Champagne Butterfield
Crown & Covenant Publications
7408 Penn Avenue
Pittsburgh, PA 15208
www.crownandcovenant.com

Third Printing, 2016

ISBN: 978-1-884527-99-9
ePub: 978-1-943017-00-3
Kindle: 978-1-943017-01-0

Library of Congress Control Number: 2015932892

Printed in the United States of America

The publisher has abbreviated or altered several names in this book to protect the privacy of certain individuals.

Cover and graphics by Eileen Bechtold. Copyediting by Rebecca Byers and Shelby Winkel. Text is set in Stempel Garamond 11 on 14 and headers in Corki Regular. Photograph by Neil Boyd Photography, Raleigh, N.C.

Unless otherwise indicated, all Scripture quotations taken from the New American Standard Bible®, Copyright © 1960, 1962, 1963, 1968, 1971, 1972, 1973, 1975, 1977, 1995 by The Lockman Foundation. Used by permission. (www.Lockman.org) Scripture quotations marked (NKJV) taken from the New King James Version®. Copyright © 1982 by Thomas Nelson. Used by permission. All rights reserved. Scripture quotations marked (ESV) are from ESV® Bible (The Holy Bible, English Standard Version®), copyright © 2001 by Crossway, a publishing ministry of Good News Publishers. Used by permission. All rights reserved.

For Ken and Floy Smith, faithful pastor and pastor's wife

Table of Contents

Preface

Conversion, Identity, Community

The book of Acts is a majestic tour de force when read in one sitting. It is one of my favorite books to gobble down all at once. By the time I finish the last two verses, I sigh with undaunted love for my Lord, dependence on the Holy Spirit for all insight and comfort, a renewed sense of God's righteousness, and a deeper yearning to understand my Bible, this book that unfolds the character of God and the unsearchable depths of his wisdom.

These are the lines that crown the book of Acts: "And [Paul] stayed two full years in his own rented quarters and was welcoming all who came to him, preaching the kingdom of God and teaching concerning the Lord Jesus Christ with all *openness, unhindered*" (Acts 28:30–31; italics added).

Beaten, shipwrecked, maligned, and betrayed, the apostle Paul arrived at an intense place of union with Christ where he was open and unhindered in all aspects of his life: struggles, identity, purity, evangelism, and hospitality. He was open and unhindered, even as he was hurt, misunderstood, abused, and lonely. In Paul's words, "We are afflicted in every way, but not crushed; perplexed, but not despairing; persecuted, but not forsaken; struck down, but not destroyed" (2 Cor. 4:8–9). In spite of the "but nots" the matter still stands: committing your life to Christ is dangerous business. The unbearable trials did not thwart Paul because, through the power of the Holy Spirit, he applied faith to his pain. By so doing, he drew close to the Lord, who knows our pain better than we do.

The book you hold in your hands, *Openness Unhindered*, takes its impetus from the last two words of the book of Acts. The Lord has used those two words in my life (and the vast world of the Bible, the God-won creation, and the redemption it unpacks) to redeem struggles, renew hope, remake purity, re-plot purpose, and recreate community. I have come to understand "openness, unhindered" as tidings that, in their biblical context, outline Christ's posture for the forgiveness of sexual sin and the renewal that he gives to the body and the mind. My prayer is that this book will serve as a bridge to Christ for those of us whose sin (sexual and otherwise) has clobbered us more times than we can count, and for our churches and Christian friends who want to help but don't know where to begin or what to say.

Hold nothing back from God.

Openness implies that we hold nothing back from the God who made us and will take care of us. We give him our heart, our desires, our hopes, our dreams, our struggles, our doubts, our fears, and our identity. We are open to God. Wide open. This kind of intimacy and trust is unsettling to us in our natural or unconverted self, especially as post-Freudian thinkers who have become both jaded and seduced by the authorizing discourses of personal experience, believing, as we all tend to do, that our feelings (especially the fixed ones) are themselves vestiges of truth.

Unhindered means that we are unencumbered by our failures; that is, we do not keep record of the countless times that we have failed God in sin, failed our friends in carelessness, and failed our own conscience by willfully disobeying the God who loves us. Instead of recordkeeping, we pray for the gift to repent of our sin at its foundation. We pray for the gift of God that redeems our mind, allowing us to see not through eyes of flesh, but rather through eyes remade by the Holy Spirit. Instead of remembering our already and often-repented sin, we remember God's covenant with us in Christ, and Christ's faithfulness.

If we are in Christ, then Christ lives in our place. He took our place on the cross and he fulfills our place today. He breathes life, purity, and redemption into our relationships, our communities, and our futures. Less of me. More of him. In Christ, I am no longer a slave to self, sin, and selfishness. In Christ, I am no longer alone. This does not, however, mean that I call sin by any other name. The law of God is my tutor, because it shows me God's will, prohibits sin, exposes my failings, and enlists me in the school of Christ.

"Redeem" is a verb of empowerment.[1] Think about how much depth and grace is packed into this little word! Roll these promises over in your heart. This is the sweet gift of Christ to his redeemed people, to those who have been both rescued from captivity and to whom the promise is performed. Christ alone does this. We violate those we love when we try to supplant Christ by trying to fill his role, or by removing ourselves from this lavish outpouring of love by refusing to take God's point of view on the matter of sin—its nature, origin, and consequences. Christ loves his people best. We cannot love as he did. We cannot suffer as he did. We cannot redeem our lives, our worlds, or our relationships.

> Redeem (Latin, *redimo*)— to obtain, purchase, ransom, liberate, rescue from captivity, pay the penalty of, and perform what has been promised.

This implies some important things. First, God's story as captured in the Bible is not a myth. It is an organizing, true narrative of who God is, what he has done, and what he will accomplish. God's story is about God. God's story precedes me. It came before me. Because it precedes my consciousness, it explains me. Because Christ redeemed me, I can apply faith in Christ to the facts of my life[2] without violating the integrity of the one or the other. In Christ, faith does not erase facts, but it does illuminate them. In Christ, God's story helps me to tell you where I hurt. God's story is our *ontology*: it explains our nature, our essence, our beginnings and our endings, our qualities, and our attributes. When we daily read our Bibles, in large chunks of whole books at a time, we daily learn that our own story began globally and ontologically. God has known us longer than anyone else has. The Bible declares that he knew us from before the foundations of the world. One of my favorite writers, William Gurnall, says that God carried us "long into the womb of His eternal purpose."[3] So God carries us, yes. But God also calls us to act and to serve.

Why is sexual sin so hard to deal with? Because often sexual sin becomes a sin of identity. One goal of this book is to help you face your sin in Christ, know your status in Christ if you have committed your life to him, and reject any identity that Christ has not prepared for you.

"We are all sexual sinners."

While this book is not exclusively about sexual sin, because sexual sin has been for me a snare whose consequences I bear, I offer many examples in the pages that follow. Sin and sexuality are not unrelated. Sam Allberry put it best: "We need to be clear, not just that we are all sinners, but that we are all sexual sinners."[4] Indeed, sin and sexuality go together like peanut butter and chocolate. They always have. But the growing disregard for and rejection of biblical norms for law and life have created a vortex of sexual sin.

As I have traveled to different churches and colleges to speak about biblical sexuality, I have met countless people for whom every vital relationship has been marred by sexual sin. I have met wives whose husbands have pornography addictions, whose teenage children engage in forwarding sexually explicit pictures on text messages, whose best friends frequent explicit cyber-sex sites and engage in cutting and mutilation. I have met husbands whose Bible-believing wives have left them for lesbian lovers. I have met teenagers who are in sexual relationships with their biological cousins and who believe that they have GSA (genetic sexual attraction). I have met preteen girls, homeschooled and protected their whole lives, who found violent pornography on their moms' cell phones and who cannot go back to any place of safety and peace. I met one woman who had had seven abortions, who goes to church weekly, and who lives a double life. For each of these people, the sense of being out of control is overwhelming. For the parents and loved ones (the secondary victims), the shame, guilt, and secret-keeping is unbearable.

Where do we go with problems of this magnitude? Is the Bible relevant, or is it a quaint and archaic moral code only useful in yesterday's world? How do we discern the brokenness of our sexuality, and how do we use the Bible to diagnose the problem and outline the solution? Do I accept the verdict of my sin at the cross? How can this be sin if it feels so good? What do I do when I am trapped like prey by the predatory nature of my own sexual sin? These are many of the questions that I address here.

This book is meant to help you peer through the keyhole of faith to see what a glorious future God promises to those in Christ, and to see that it is never too late for you or anyone else. Christ redeems. Even our struggles, our failures, and our suffering are redemptive in Christ. But there is blood involved. There is a cutting off and a cutting away that redemption demands. Stepping into God's story means abandoning a deeply held desire to make meaning of our own lives on our own terms based on the preciousness of our own feelings. We leave and we cleave. Or we never really understand what it means that Christ died in our place. We can only take this leap if Christ jumps for us. While we can beg him with a contrite heart, we cannot accomplish salvation, repentance, or sanctification at our will.

In addition to the people for whom every relationship has been hijacked by sexual sin, I also have spent a bulk of my time talking with people who are struggling with unwanted homosexual desire. It has been hard for my friends in this group to get their churches to recognize that they did not choose this desire. It has been hard for my friends to be torn between the church (itself confused and divided) and the world (similarly vexed).

There seem to be three lenses through which to examine today's sexual landscape. The first views gender and sexuality as cultural artifices, not ontological, God-ordained categories. Folks with this lens reject the idea that the Bible is an inerrant (without

5

error) and inspired-by-God text, even though some claim a deep love for many parts of the Bible, and a self-identified high view of Scripture. It is not unusual to have a high but also flawed view of something. People can have a high view of something that they don't understand. I may have a high view of Shakespeare's sonnets, but if I cannot scan for iambic pentameter, I will only be able to appreciate them in a surface or "vulgar" way. Faithful readers of any text may have differing levels of literacy in discerning the meaning of those texts.

The same is true for Scripture. A high view does not guard against low literacy. To unbelievers and to those who hold to a *revisionist hermeneutic*,[5] this is the case. But the Bible unfolds its own hermeneutic, as God himself determines how we should approach him. Of course you can read the Bible through a lens other than that which God asks, but you will never know the God of Scripture through his written Word if you do.

> Revisionist hermeneutic — a reading practice that questions and reconceives the Bible's plain meaning and the shared testimony of the church.

God's created order includes norms, boundaries, definitions, and limits for sexuality and gender, some of which may be difficult to embrace, especially if your personal experience puts you at odds with people you love and care about. Bible-believing Christians are gender and sexuality *essentialists*, believing that there is an essence to maleness and femaleness, and that God's created order mandates sexual union exclusively between one man and one woman in the covenant of biblical marriage. To the rest of the world, such essentialist understandings of sexuality, gender, and selfhood are reactionary, backward, and dangerous.[6] To the rest of the world, the Bible-believing Christian's rejection of the wisdom of the world in favor of the fear of God and allegiance to the thousands-of-years-old Bible is foolish and hate-mongering. I completely understand how these folks feel and interpret this. And my shift from postmodern intellectual, unbelieving professor, and lesbian activist to repentant Bible-believing Christian has tagged me a dangerous idiot. I love the folks in the former group. This group holds my former family of choice, and the learning community they cherish and inhabit is the one I helped build. Unbelievers tend to be pragmatists about morality. If consenting adults are hurting no one and cherishing what they have together, they are deemed to have a good relationship. I believed this for many years and I understand where they are coming from.

The second lens through which to read sexuality is with an inerrant, inspired, and dependable Bible. But even when we use the right lens, we also use the eyes of flesh, so we won't get good results. In this group we find

> Inerrancy—without error and therefore completely true and trustworthy.
>
> Inspiration—God-breathed, supernatural, holy.

Christians who uphold what we call the *inerrancy* and *inspiration* of Scripture, but have never struggled with homoerotic desires themselves, looked deeply enough into Scripture, or listened well enough to their friends who do struggle. These folks unbiblically believe that the struggle is the sin. They do not know how to approach their Lesbian, Gay, Bisexual, and Transgender (LGBT) neighbors because deep down they truly believe that if gay people would just come to Jesus, they would all be straight.

Recently someone in my extended church community asked if the lesbian daughter of a mutual friend of ours was going to commit her life to Jesus and "go straight." I reminded the churchy lady (I live in the South, so indulge me here) that the young woman she mentioned had made a profession of faith, and I had no more knowledge of whether she would develop heterosexual attractions than I did if she was going to buy a puppy at the state fair this year.

Homoerotic desire, these folks believe, is rooted in willful sin, bad choice-making, full-blown lust, and/or lack of knowledge of or real faith in Jesus. Without intending it, they endorse a prosperity gospel about sexuality, one that falsely believes that Christ died on a cross and rose again to make you happy and prosperous on earth. We all make choices along the path of our life journeys, but if sin is only about bad choice-making, we don't need a savior. Sin is bigger and deeper and longer than bad choice-making. All sin is a vestige of the fall and a transgression against God, but that doesn't mean that patterns of temptation are themselves proof that we are actively sinning. While it is true that in conversion we are new creatures in Christ, it is also true that on this side of the resurrection we will struggle with all manner of sin, including, if God permits, homoerotic desire. That is the kicker, and I hear this all the time: "God would never make someone with a homosexual baseline." Really? Original Sin means that we are born in fallenness—both moral (which requires the sanctifying power of God through saving faith) and natural (which requires medical or supernatural healing, but not necessarily saving or sanctifying faith). Sexuality can straddle this line, as sometimes sexual dysfunction results from natural fallenness (such as intersexuality, being born with reproductive or sexual anatomy of both sexes). So yes, we are all "born this way." And even after we are born again, we will all struggle with sin until we die and enter Glory or Jesus returns.

It is not the absence of sin that makes you a believer.

Whether the pain you face now is the consequence of your sin or the sin of others, in God's providence and in saving faith, Romans 8:28 still reigns: "God causes all things to work together for good to those who love God, to those who are called according to His purpose." It is not the absence of sin that makes you a believer. It is the presence of Christ in the midst of your struggle that commends the believer and sets you apart in the world. Real conversion gives you Christ's company as you walk through the valley of the shadow of death. Indeed, the fall made everything— including my deepest desires—fall. And this happened under God's providential eye, not behind his back.

The third lens is used by those who believe they have Christ's saving grace, but do not believe that God calls them to repent of all sin, in part because they use the wrong biblical lens. They believe that there are holes in the biblical story, holes that can only be filled by the "moral logic" of personal experience or the culture in which we live. These people believe in Jesus, but extract him from the Word of God by suggesting that we have new and improved ways of understanding the human condition.

While the Bible is not a science book and will not tell me how to fix my computer or build a telescope, it is spot-on when it comes to the moral condition of humanity. When folks in this group claim Christ's confidence, but uphold a hermeneutic that unwittingly but wholeheartedly erases Jesus' brutal sacrifice for sin, they often do so on the grounds of new evidence about morality that changes what the Bible means. Every generation seems to arrive at new evidence to explain away a biblical truth. Part of loving your sister or brother involves holding the mirror of Scripture up to the reflection of personal testimony. If personal testimony does not reflect the Bible's account of a life of faith and repentance, then for the sake of your friend and for the sake of Christ's witness, bring the Word of life to bear upon the claim of conversion.

My hope is that *Openness Unhindered* may help in this humble quest. Jesus cannot be separated from the whole Bible; and the Old Testament is not dispensable, or with it the moral law of God.[7] For my friends in this group, I want to say thank you for hanging in there with me.

Being born in Adam means that we cannot escape *Original Sin*: we are born with a primary desire to do evil, and a primal propensity to enjoy in the flesh what God calls sin. Original Sin makes us not just bad, but blind. This fact—that Original Sin distorts us at the deepest level—can be an overwhelming idea. But that is not its intent. Original Sin is not meant to shame anyone. Rather, the doctrine of Original Sin is the most democratizing idea in all of human history. It means that we are all in the same boat. And if we are in Christ, no pattern or sin or brokenness defines us. Christ's virgin birth represents, in spite of all the hoopla around Christmas, his humiliation, not his exaltation.

Original Sin—the sinful nature that we all inherit because of Adam's fall.

We who are broken by sin cling to and identify with Christ's humiliation, a key Christian virtue and posture. But Christ is no longer humiliated. He sits at God's right hand, interceding for us as we run the race set before us. Repentance unto life means that we must repent of sin, even sins of identity. There is no shame in this. I know this sounds counterintuitive. As you enter into the section of *Openness Unhindered* that addresses identity, some of this material may be dense and foreign. Bear with me, please. You can take the professor out of the university classroom, but sometimes you can't take the university classroom out of the professor!

Take my hand and join me on this journey, please. If you are a Christian and you are struggling with sexual sin, this book is meant to equip and encourage you in your daily walk of faith with Jesus. If you are not yet a Christian, my hope is that I can reach through the pages of this book, take your hand, and put it in the hand of our Savior.

If you call yourself a Christian, but you do not believe that you need to repent of the sin that claims your identity, heart, and perhaps body, my prayer is that this book sounds a serious alarm to you. Your soul is at stake, and I will take the risk of offending you to help. Salvation is a gift, offered to all who have a broken and contrite heart (Ps. 51:17). God promises tenderness to the brokenhearted: "I will seek the lost, bring back the scattered, bind up the broken and strengthen the sick," but judgment for those who defend the right to their sin: "but the fat and the strong I will destroy. I will feed them with judgment" (Ezek. 34:16). A humble and a broken heart is a gift from God. Pray for a heart that breaks on the rock of Christ. Pray for a tender conscience about sin, even your deepest, most primal sin.

Salvation is a gift.

Salvation is a gift, and it is a good gift to pray for! What do you do with a gift? You receive it, and then you act on all the bounty that it offers. If you are the parent or spouse of someone trapped in a sexual sin that seems to have stolen your loved one from you, my hope is that you find comfort and insight in the pages that follow. Read on, please.

Conversion

The Spark of a New Identity

Welcome to my world. By day, a homeschool mom and a pastor's wife. By dark of the morning, a writer. Sometimes this perfect bubble is burst, and I get on planes and speak to church and university audiences about living a messy life in Christ. Some days, the complex tapestry of my life in Christ makes sense. Most days, though, it does not. My testimony is like iodine on starch. There is nothing neutral about it, about me, or about my life in Jesus Christ.

Of course, it is not just my testimony—the story, to the best of my ability to tell it, of how the God of the universe burst into my secular world and atheistic worldview in the person of Jesus Christ in 1999, when I was thirty-six years old, happily partnered in a lesbian relationship, and recently tenured in the English department of Syracuse University, poised and ready to work in the field of Queer Theory. Somehow, I missed the "party-like-it's-1999" paradigm, and my world was turned upside down and inside out.

I was a true believer before I became a true believer in Christ. Passionately pursuing truth and justice is in my blood.

I wrote about all of this in a book entitled *The Secret Thoughts of an Unlikely Convert*. It is a small book, and I wrote it because, as the years unfolded after my conversion, I started to look dangerously cleaned up. I'm not. Well-meaning church ladies who had been raised on the right side of the Christian tracks and who gave themselves unearned kudos for good choices thought I was one of them. In the parlance of queer culture, I "passed." But I'm not one of them. I'm Mary Magdalene. I'm Rahab the Harlot. Left to my own devices, I am much more the whore next door than the girl next door. I'm a woman with a past, and Christ's call on my life did not lobotomize me. Nor did it leave me with the sentiment that Christians are better, nicer, more honest and a more fun crop of cronies. We are not. No way. At least, not in my experience.

My conversion left my former friends and family thinking I was loony to the core. How could I leave a worldview that was open, welcoming, and inclusive for one that believes in Original Sin, values the law of God, seeks conversion into a born-again constitution, believes in the truthful ontology of God's Word as found in the Bible, claims the exclusivity of Christ for salvation, and purports the redemptive quality of suffering? Only one reason: because Jesus is a real and risen Lord and because he claimed me for himself.

Life stories are messy, contradictory, and humiliating. Mine is.

I wrote *Openness Unhindered* as much to learn as I did to share what I have learned in the years since the publication of *Secret Thoughts*. If you are curious about Christianity, it is my hope that this book answers your questions about who Jesus is and what Christians believe. If you are struggling with your sin, trying to apply God's expectations and the balm of his purpose to each clobbering temptation, my hope is that these pages will encourage you to fight the good fight, for the honor of Jesus is at stake in every encounter, every thought, every relationship, every decision. If you have lost the fight and now believe that the Bible and the God who stands behind it cannot be trusted, I hope that you will find in the pages of this book the humiliating reality that we don't measure up, and that it is never too late to repent—again—and turn back to the God who made you. Jesus understands you better than you understand yourself. Please take my hand and join me on this journey.

For those of you who missed *Secret Thoughts*, let me share a little about myself.

I had a normal childhood. I was raised in the Catholic faith, and I attended, predominantly, liberal Catholic schools.

My liberal, Catholic, all-girl high school discipled me in the life skills that I use today. I learned there to read deeply and well, to diagram a sentence before I tried to interpret it, and to look out for the unloved and draw them in. I also learned that the Bible was a literary text, discernible through the lenses of literary devices. It seemed to me that the resurrection of Jesus Christ was a metaphor, powerful only in worlds of words. I loved worlds of words, and so a metaphorical god with metaphorical power was good enough for me. God was simply another manifestation of the power of positive thinking, at least for me.

I had a heterosexual adolescence.

My all-girl Catholic high school dished out plenty of academic rigor and ably prepared me for college, but it did not prepare me for the sexual meat market that I met there.

I had a clear love-hate relationship with this sexual meat market.

On the one hand, I was jazzed by the attention that college men gave me. I had always been a nerd, easy to overlook, a plain Jane. But I started to blossom in college, and people noticed. On the other hand, this sexual meat market made me feel ill inside. As I courted the attention of men, I fantasized about relationships with women.

In college, I met my first boyfriend. It was a heady experience. But we graduated and it was then that I noticed it: an undercurrent of longing inserted itself into my intense friendships with women. This intrigued me, so I followed the rabbit trail.

I could not manage to contain or make sense of sexuality. It completely bowled me over. I have never felt so out of control, so metaphorically intoxicated as I did during my twenties, when the sexual backdrop of college and then graduate school mixed with my own tangled sexual desires brought this onslaught of confusion, euphoria, and chaos.

From the age of twenty-two until twenty-eight, I continued to date men and at the same time feel a sense of longing and connection that toppled over the edges for my women friends, especially my friends from my growing lesbian and feminist community base.

I never hated men. They just didn't show up on my radar in ways as meaningful, deep, or important. I never dreamed of marriage or kids. I presumed that I was straight. Men liked me. I tolerated sexual advances. And I remained steadfastly curious about what it would be like to be with a woman.

This repetitious lesbian sensibility rooted and grew: I simply preferred the company of women. In my late twenties, enhanced by feminist philosophy and LGBT political advocacy, my homosocial preference morphed into homosexuality. That shift was subtle, not startling. My lesbian identity and my love for my LGBT community developed in sync with my lesbian sexual practice. Life finally came together for me and made sense.

I studied Sigmund Freud. I cheered that the *Diagnostic and Statistical Manual of Mental Disorders* had long since removed homosexuality from its list of disorders (thus rendering homosexuality, in the eyes of the world and the academy, normal). With no prohibitions or constraints, by the time I had graduated from Ohio State with my PhD in English literature and critical theory, I left the Buckeye State with my first lesbian partner. We moved to New York for me to begin a tenure track position in the English department of Syracuse University. It was 1992.

My life as a lesbian seemed normal. I considered it an enlightened, chosen path. Lesbianism felt like a cleaner and more moral sexual practice.[1] Always preferring symmetry to asymmetry, I believed I had found my real self. Many other women in my lesbian community had had a heterosexual season. We believed that was because heterosexuality had become, in the words of the late lesbian poet and English professor Adrienne Rich, compulsory. When I fell in love with a woman for the first time, I thought I had found my real self. I was hooked, and I had no intention of looking back.

What happened to my Catholic training? I believed now that faith in God was superstitious and intellectually untenable.

The name Jesus, which had rolled off my tongue in a little girl's prayers, then rolled off my back in college, now made me recoil with anger.

As a professor of English and women's studies, I cared about morality, justice, and compassion. As a scholar of the nineteenth century, fervent for the worldviews of Freud, Hegel, Marx, and Darwin, I strove to stand with the disempowered. My life at this time was happy, meaningful, and full.

My next lesbian partner and I shared many vital interests: AIDS activism, children's health and literacy, golden retriever rescue, and our Unitarian Universalist church, to name a few. It was hard to argue that she and I were anything but good citizens and caregivers. The LGBT community values hospitality and applies it with skill, sacrifice, and integrity. Indeed, I honed the hospitality gifts that I use today as a pastor's wife in my queer community.

I began researching the Religious Right and their politics of hatred against people like me. To do this, I began reading the Bible while looking for some Bible scholar to help me wade through this complex book. I took note that the Bible was an engaging literary display of every genre and trope and type. It had edgy poetry, deep and complex philosophy, and compelling narrative stories. It also embodied a worldview that I hated. Sin. Repentance. Sodom and Gomorrah. Absurd.

At this time, the Promise Keepers came to town and parked their little circus at the university. In my war against stupid, I wrote an article published in the local newspaper. It was 1997.

A lot of Christians hated that article, and many wrote letters to me about how I was going to hell. One letter, from Ken Smith, was different from the rest. I liked its tone. And its author was a neighbor. I responded to this one letter, and Ken and I became friends. Real friends. Not friendship evangelism. I was not a project to Ken. I was a neighbor, and Ken taught me that Christians value neighbors.

Ken's letter didn't mock; it engaged.

With the letter, Ken initiated two years of bringing the church to me. Oh, I had seen my share of Bible verses on placards at gay pride marches. That Christians who mocked me at Gay Pride Day were happy that I and everyone I loved were going to hell was as clear as the sky is blue. But Ken's letter did not mock; it engaged. So when he invited me to dinner at his house to discuss these matters more fully, I accepted. My motives at the time were clear: surely this would be good for my research.

Something else happened. Ken and his wife, Floy, and I became friends. They entered my world. They met my friends. We did book exchanges. We talked openly about sexuality and politics. They did not act as if such conversations were polluting them. They did not treat me like a blank slate.

When we ate together, Ken prayed in a way that I had never heard before. His prayers were intimate. Vulnerable. He repented of his sin in front of me. He thanked God for all things. Ken's God was holy and firm, yet full of mercy. At my first meal at their home, Ken and Floy omitted two important steps in the rulebook of how Christians should deal with a heathen like me: 1) they did not share the gospel with me, and 2) they did not invite me to church. Because of these omissions to the Christian rulebook as I had come to know it, I felt that when Ken extended his hand to me in friendship, it was safe to close my hand in his.

I started meeting with Ken and Floy regularly, reading the Bible in earnest, with pen in hand and notebook in lap. I read the way a glutton devours. I became close friends with a member of the church, a man my age with my complex history of sexual sin, but who had made a profession of faith and had become a follower of this man-God Jesus. He helped me along with my Bible reading and questions. I started to read the Bible the way that I was trained to read a book, examining its textual authority, authorship, *canonicity*, and internal hermeneutics. A year later, this man and I became engaged (long story here, and you will have to read *Secret Thoughts* to get the fuller one). When he dumped me, that was when I knew that I belonged to Christ alone. I will be ever grateful for this face-plant of a lesson, but also for what he

Canonicity—refers to the books inspired by God for inclusion in the Bible.

Hermeneutics—the method of interpreting the Bible.

modeled for me: how to read the Bible, in big chunks, reading it from Genesis to Revelation many times in one year.

I read the Bible like that the first year, arguing with its gender politics and its statements about slavery. But I kept reading it. Slowly and over time, the Bible started to take on a life and meaning that startled me. Some of my well-worn paradigms no longer stuck. As I studied the Bible, I found answers to my initial accusations. I delved into its canonicity, its hermeneutics, and its opposing theological approaches. My PhD training ably prepared me to know what a book says, to assess the integrity of its textual history and canonicity, and to make a call about its authority. God used this singular nerdy skill in the most important book study of my life.

The Bible simultaneously encouraged and enraged me.

The Bible was this unmined text, and it simultaneously encouraged and enraged me.

I had to at least ponder the hermeneutical claim that this book was different from all the others because it was inspired by a holy God and was inherently true and trustworthy. This led me to go through the presuppositional truth-claims, just to check the math of the meaning here. The logic claim starts with God's attributes, particularly his goodness and his holiness and authority.

1) *God's goodness.* If God is good, then his goodness is unrestrained by time and therefore anticipates and guards against the ill treatment of any people group. This was a book written by men who claimed to be inspired by the Holy Spirit. I noticed that its statements about sin were followed by offers of repentance and forgiveness. God deals differently with us when we deal differently with him.

2) *God's holiness and authority.* If God is the creator of all things, and if the Bible has his seal of truth and power, then the Bible has the right to interrogate my life and my culture, and not the other way around. If this was a book written by men who were inspired by the Holy Spirit, then its admonitions about sin were not applied cultural phobia. Indeed, prior to

reading the Bible for myself, I believed that the category of sin was merely applied cultural phobia. But even as a postmodern reader, I understood the idea that authority can depend only on that which is higher than itself. If God exists, then who is higher than God? I wondered.

My friends knew that I was reading the Bible. First, the dean of the chapel took me out to lunch and shared his belief that the Old Testament was dispensable and, with it, any prohibition about sexuality and immorality. But I had been reading and studying the three different narratives of the Old Testament, and it seemed to me that you couldn't dispense with it in its entirety without violating a foundational rule about canonicity: no creating canons within canons. In fact, I had just gone over this in my graduate seminar in Queer Theory and it made me wonder if the chapel dean ought not sit in on my class. His position seemed like a hermeneutic of convenience, tailoring the text to fit my experience, and not a hermeneutic of integrity, where the text gets the chance to fulfill its internal mission.

Queer Theory—a branch of gay and lesbian studies developed in 1990; emphasizes the social construction of gender and sexuality.

Even a postmodern reader-response critic knows that each text has an internal mission. The internal mission of the Bible is to transform the nature of humanity. That is why unbelievers know it is a dangerous text. I was puzzled that the chapel dean seemed to have such little understanding of this book that he had studied better than I had. It confirmed for me what all English professors suspect about the world: no one really knows how to read a book anymore.

Next, at a dinner gathering that my partner and I were hosting, my transgendered friend J cornered me in the kitchen. She put her large hand over mine and said, "Rosaria, this Bible reading is changing you."

I felt exposed. She was right. She always was. "But what if it is true? What if Jesus is a real and risen Lord? What if we are all in trouble?" I asked.

J exhaled deeply and sat down in the chair across from mine. Her eyes looked wise and she said: "Rosaria, I was a Presbyterian minister for fifteen years. I prayed that God would heal me, but he didn't. If you want, I will pray for you."

This encounter gave me secret tacit permission to keep reading the Bible. My dear friend J had also read it cover to cover, many times, and had rooted around in its deep crevices for life purpose and help. The bomb she dropped also enraged me. Who is this Jesus who heals some but not others? No peace and social justice activist wants an unequal-opportunity God.

The next day, when I returned home from work, I found two large milk crates spilling over with theological books. J's books. She was giving them to me. In Calvin's *Institutes of the Christian Religion*, in the margins of a passage about the book of Romans, in J's handwriting, was a warning: "Be careful here. Don't forget Romans 1."

This is what it says in Romans 1:

> *21 For even though they knew God, they did not honor Him as God or give thanks, but they became futile in their speculations and their foolish heart was darkened.*
> *22 Professing to be wise, they became fools,*
> *23 and exchanged the glory of the incorruptible God for an image in the form of corruptible man and of birds and four-footed animals and crawling creatures.*
> *24 Therefore God gave them over in the lusts of their hearts to impurity, so that their bodies would be dishonored among them.*
> *25 For they exchanged the truth of God for a lie, and worshiped and served the creature rather than the Creator....*
> *26 For this reason God gave them over to degrading passions; for their women exchanged the natural function for that which is unnatural....*

I found the verb clauses here to be particularly arresting—did not honor God, did not give thanks, engaged in futile speculations, became fools, exchanged the incorruptible for the corruptible. God gives us over to our lusts: when we look at the world through our lusts we dishonor our bodies and worship the world. This verse seemed to provide a haunting literary echo to Genesis 3, where Eve's desire to live independently of God's authority made perfect sense to me. If I were Eve, I would have done the same thing. And at the same time Eve's, and then Adam's, seemingly innocent sin served as the leverage for the whole world to come tumbling down, fierce and fast, bloody and brilliant.

The two chapters, one in Genesis and one in Romans, stood out as bookends of my life. But not just my life. That is the rub. The Bible declares itself an owner's manual of the human race. While I loathed this description, a little part of me was starting to see how Genesis 3 and Romans 1 stood out as the table of contents of what ails the world. Indeed, Romans 1 does not end by highlighting homosexuality as the worst and most extreme example of the sin of failing to give God the glory for creating us. Here is where this passage finds its crescendo:

> 29 being filled with all unrighteousness, wickedness, greed, evil; full of envy, murder, strife, deceit, malice; they are gossips,
> 30 slanderers, haters of God, insolent, arrogant, boastful, inventors of evil; disobedient to parents,
> 31 without understanding, untrustworthy, unloving, unmerciful;
> 32 and although they know the ordinance of God, that those who practice such things are worthy of death, they not only do the same, but also give hearty approval to those who practice them.

Homosexuality, then, is not the end-point of the problem, for God or for the world. But it is presented here as one step in the journey. Homosexuality seemed then consequential, not causal. Homosexuality, from God's point of view, is an identity-rooted ethical outworking of Original Sin. Thousands of years before I was born, in the garden, when sin entered the world,

Adam's fall rendered my deep and primal feelings untrustworthy and untrue. According to the Bible itself, homosexuality—and the heterosexual sexual sin that I had committed—was not the root of all sin, not even the root of my sin. Romans had already cinched it for me: sexual sin is a fruit of something larger than its own desire.

I had taught, studied, read, and lived a very different notion of homosexuality.

For the first time in my life, I wondered if I was wrong.

This stopped me in my tracks.

Somehow it was easier to hate the Bible when it squared off against me. When it seemed to arbitrarily single me out and oppress or marginalize me and people like me, it was easy to dismiss. But now that it was getting under my skin it became a foe of a different and more menacing kind.

I tried to toss the Bible and its teachings in the trash. I really tried. But Ken encouraged me to keep reading. I trusted him, and so I did.

As I read and reread the Bible, I kept catching my wings in its daily embrace. I was fighting the idea that the Bible is inspired and inerrant—that is, that its meaning and purpose have a holy and supernatural authority that has protected it over the years of its canonicity, and that it is the repository of truth. How could a smart cookie like me embrace these things? I didn't even believe in truth. I was a postmodernist. I believed in truth claims. I believed that the reader constructed the text—that a text's meaning found its power only in the reader's interpretation of it. As I told my students over and over again, without the reader, a book is just paper and glue. How could this one book lay claim to a birthright and progeny different from all others?

As I was reading and discussing these things with Ken, he pointed out to me that Jesus is the Word made flesh, and that "knowing Jesus" demands embracing the Jesus of the Bible, not the Jesus of someone's imagination. The whole Bible. Even the places that took my life captive.

I straddled two worlds and two lives for two years. Some days, I felt like the worst of all hypocrites. And that's because I was. Other days, I felt like a true liberal, truly loving and abiding with people who were so different from me. And this was true, too.

Was I double-minded? Was I counting the costs? Yes. To both.

The Bible got to be bigger inside me than I.

After years and years of this, something happened. The Bible got to be bigger inside me than I.

It overflowed into my world.

I fought against it with all my might.

Then, one Sunday morning, two years after I first met Ken and Floy and two years after I started reading the Bible for my research, I left the bed I shared with my partner and an hour later sat in a pew at the Syracuse Reformed Presbyterian Church. I say this not to be lurid, but to remind us that we never know the treacherous path that others take to arrive in the pew that we share Lord's Day after Lord's Day. Conspicuous in my appearance, I reminded myself that I came there to meet God, not fit in.

The first sermon that I heard Ken preach was intended for children. *Whew*, I thought. *This is just my speed.* Ken started to talk about the narrow gate and the wide gate and made a big deal about some silly prop that was in his pocket. I didn't get that part. Actually, I didn't get much of the sermon. My mind kept wandering to last year's gay pride march, wide as it was with people just like me. That made me wonder: why does my mind keep traveling to the wide path?

I kept going back to church to hear more sermons. I had made friendships with people in the church by this time, and I appreciated the way that they talked about the sermons throughout the week, how the Word of God dwelt in them, how they referenced it in the details of their days. English professors by training love cross-texting, and I muddled over this in my mind: cross-texting the Bible with your life places you inside God's story, God's ontology. Is this safe? Is this deadly? I pondered these matters.

Ken was preaching through the gospel of Matthew, with its bewildering cast of characters and problems, unsuspecting folks "separated unto the gospel," seeds choked by the world, feeding thousands with some poor and nameless kid's bread and fish, then Jesus' cutting question to impetuous Peter, "Do you still lack understanding?" (Matt. 15:16).

One Lord's Day, Pastor Ken just stopped there, turned his steel blue eyes on the congregation, and held a long pause before he turned this question on us: "Congregation: Did Christ ever say this to you?" This startled me. This was my question. This question was for me: *Do I still lack understanding?* Who is speaking here, the man behind the pulpit or the God-man behind the foundation and redemption of his people?

There was something about the hermeneutic of preaching that disarmed me. Indeed, even after all of these years, it still does.

The image of me and everyone I loved suffering in hell crashed over me like shark-infested waves of a raging sea. Suffering in hell not because we were gay, but because we were proud. We wanted to be autonomous. It was our hearts first, and our bodies followed. I got it. I heard it. Finally.

I counted the costs and I did not like the math.

This was my crucible, and this is my crucible: if the Bible is true, I was dead. If the Bible is false, I am the biggest fool on earth.

But God's promises rolled in like another round of waves into my world. One Lord's Day, Ken was preaching on John 7:17: "If anyone wills to do [God's] will, he shall know concerning the doctrine" (NKJV). This verse exposed the quicksand in which my feet were stuck. I was a thinker. I was paid to read books and write about them. I expected that, in all areas of my life, understanding came before obedience, not the other way around. I wanted God to show me, on my terms, why homosexuality was a sin. I wanted to be the judge, not the one being judged.

Perhaps, I thought, like Eve in the garden, I wanted to eat of the Tree of the Knowledge of Good and Evil so that I could become and replace God. I wondered. Hadn't I already done this? Hadn't we all? If my consciousness fell in Adam's sin, as the Bible purports, no wonder I couldn't think my way out of this quandary. This wasn't a game of thinking and the matching of wits. Could my heart echo God's call for obedience? Could I "will to do God's will," just this once? The stakes were so very high. They always are.

But the verse promised understanding after obedience. I wrestled with the question: Did I really want to understand homosexuality from God's point of view, or did I just want to argue with him?

I prayed that night that God would give me the willingness to obey before I understood. Starting with my own sexuality was too scary, too impossible. So I started with Jesus. I prayed that God would be pleased to reveal his Son in me. I prayed that I would be a vessel of Jesus. I prayed that God would make me a godly woman—and then I laughed out loud at the insanity of this prayer. I prayed that God would give me the faith to repent of my sin at its foundation. What is the root of my sin?

How does one repent of a sin that doesn't feel like sin?

How does one repent of a sin that doesn't feel like sin at all, but rather a normal not-bothering-another-soul kind of life? How had I come to this place? What is the root of the sin of sexual identity? Being a lesbian was not just a description of the kind of sex I liked to have. Being a lesbian encompassed a whole range of feelings and perception, character qualities, and sensibilities. It reflected the depth of my nonsexual friendships and the integrated community I wanted to build with women. Being a lesbian also reflected the kind of professor I was, the classes I taught, the books I read, and the dissertations I directed. I was all in. And, I was a jumble of emotions, because according to the Bible, what I called community, God called idolatry.

I did not know what to do, so I prayed the way I had heard Ken pray. He often would call upon the Lord to teach him this or that. So I prayed that the Lord would help me to see my life from his point of view. It was then that I noticed it: as I looked around my house, I had dozens of *PRIDE* posters, T-shirts, coffee mugs.

The flag that waved in the breeze at my porch was a *PRIDE* flag. Pride had become my best friend. In the LGBT world, we defined *pride* as a healthy self-esteem. But something started to crack a little and I dared to just ask the question: was I domesticating a tiger? Without gay pride, where would I be? Where would any of us be? In the LGBT community, the opposite of pride is self-hatred. But in the Bible, the opposite of pride is faith. Was pride keeping me from faith, or was pride keeping me from self-hatred? That was when the question inserted itself like a foot in the door: Did pride distort self-esteem the way lust distorts love? This was the first of my many betrayals against the LGBT community: whose dictionary did I trust? The one used by the community that I helped create or the one that reflected the God who created me? As soon as the question formed itself into words, I felt convicted of the sin of pride. Pride was my downfall. I asked God for the mercy to repent of my pride at its root.

The next morning, when I looked in the mirror, I looked the same. But when I looked in the mirror of the Bible, I wondered: who am I? Am I an atheist? Am I a lesbian? Do I have to have a category? Has this life of my own invention merely been a case of mistaken identity? The strongest sense of self I had at the time was my lesbian identity, but even that was pieced together by a jumble of things. If Jesus could split the world asunder, divide the soul and the spirit, judge the thoughts and intentions of the heart, could he make my true identity prevail? Who am I? Who will God have me be?

I still felt like a lesbian in my body and heart. That was, I felt, my real identity. But what is my *true* identity? The Bible makes clear that the real and the true have a troubled relationship on this side of eternity. For many people in the Bible, their true identity and calling comes only after a long struggle, with God, with wilderness, and with dreams and hopes and plans. The Bible makes clear that my future and my calling always echo an attribute of God. Obedience constrains; it always mirrors suffering, as every selection implies a sacrifice. What is bigger? My lesbian identity and the feminist and postmodern worldview that fuels it, or God's authority over me and holy sovereignty over the world?

Who is this Jesus?

Did I know him?

Did I still lack understanding?

Could I trust him?

Then, one ordinary day, I came to Jesus. No altar calls in a Reformed Presbyterian Church, so no fanfare or manipulation. We were singing from Psalm 119:56: "This is mine because forever all Thy precepts I preserve." After I sang these words, I checked them in the Bible, just to be sure that the psalter didn't have some tricky misprint in it. The Bible used a helping verb and noted the verse like this: "this has become mine." Something about that helping verb made something shift in me. Two weight-bearing retaining walls collapsed in my mind. The first wall came crashing down because I had just sung condemnation unto myself. This Bible was not mine. I had scorned it and cursed it and despised it. But I had been reading and rereading this book, and the use of the helping verb (*has* in "has become") troubled me. Two years of laborious reading embodied the helping verb "has"; it showed process, journey, pilgrimage, and danger. But, I was not "in Christ" and therefore could not possibly keep these precepts (God's law), not in word, heart-change, or deed.

Here was the shattering of the second wall: I had read the Bible many times through, and I saw for myself that it had a holy Author; I saw for myself that it was a canonized collection of sixty-six books with a unified biblical revelation. I heard for myself that when the words "this is mine" came out of my mouth in congregational singing, I was attesting to this one, simple truth: that the line of communication that God ordained for his people required this wrestling with Scripture, and that I truly wanted both to hear God's voice breathed in my life, and I wanted God to hear my pleas.

The fog burned away. The whole Bible, each jot and tittle, was my open highway to a holy God.

My hands let go of the wheel of self-invention. I came to Jesus alone, open-handed, and naked. I had no dignity upon which to stand. As an advocate for peace and social justice, I thought that I was on the side of kindness, integrity, and care. It was thus a crushing revelation to discover that it was Jesus I had been persecuting the whole time—not just some historical figure named Jesus, but my Jesus, my Prophet, my Priest, my King, my Savior, my Redeemer, my Friend. That Jesus.

In this war of worldviews, Ken and Floy were there. A friend in the church, R, who had become my best champion, was there for me. The church who had been praying for me for years was there. Jesus triumphed. And I was a broken mess. I lost everything but the dog.

Repentance is the posture of the Christian.

Of course, there is only one thing to do when you meet the living God. You must fall on your face and repent of your sins. Repentance is bittersweet business. Repentance is not just a conversion exercise. It is the posture of the Christian. Just like a dancer's body finds its points and an equestrian incorporates her body weight into the movement of the horse, the Christian learns how to melt her will into God's. Repentance is the threshold to God. When heat meets ice, the solid substance liquefies completely. Repentance liquefies the will of the flesh. Repentance is our daily fruit, our hourly washing, our minute-by-minute wakeup call, our reminder of God's creation, Jesus' blood, and the Holy Spirit's comfort. Repentance is the only no-shame solution to a renewed Christian conscience because it proves the obvious: that God was right all along. To the sexual sinner, repentance feels like death—because it is. The "you" who once was is no longer, even if your old feelings remain.

Consciousness of sin resides not just in how you feel, but more potently in who Jesus is and what he has done. Your point of view and Christ's atonement impact like a slow-motion car crash, as you see how he satisfied God's justice for you. For me. You smell the blood and hear the agony in spurts and fits and all of a sudden you see what you could not see before: you cost Jesus everything—life, dignity, respect, peace. And he did not deserve this. Not even close. But he did more than accept this fate. He embraced it, out of love for me, and a mysterious glory that only this kind of God-love can manifest. When you step into the atonement, you are no longer a bystander. The blood is on your hands. What happens in repentance of sin is you see Jesus: "He is clothed with a robe dipped in blood, and His name is called The Word of God" (Rev. 19:13).

As I sit now at my desk and write, my kids are listening to *The Magician's Nephew* on CD. Sometimes this life that I toy with on these pages seems a million miles away. Sometimes it feels like I am truly writing about someone else. But I still see the blood. Every time I repent of sins, I behold again the inseparable blood and love. Repentance is still the threshold. Loss of identity in this idol or that is still the consequence. But new creatures in Christ manifest at times a softening amnesia. And it is fear about that amnesia that calls me to tell you more about who Jesus is. I write now about matters that happened over a decade ago. God has taken me on a long journey. But like most pilgrimages, mine engenders more questions than answers.

Questions lag and nag, even after repentance, even after all of these years. Some days I want to pass as another fifty-something church lady. But these questions vex me:

What about homosexuality? Did I ever get some special insight from the Holy Spirit as to why it is a sin? Did I immediately upon conversion (or ever) feel that "unnaturalness" about homosexual sex that Romans 1 outlines? Or as a friend recently asked me, "Rosaria, when did the 'yuck factor' about homosexual sex hit you upside the head?" (Consider this a friendly warning: if you ask me questions like this, you will end up in a book.) Well, that is not what happened. The sinfulness of sin unfolded for me in the authority of the Bible, the growing sweetness with my union with Christ, and the slow sanctification of the mind that this births. At a certain point in life, I knew that I had to turn over the wheel to God. A little like an Alzheimer's patient, who in a flashing moment of mental lucidity signs over his rights to his able-minded caregiver, a believer signs over her rights of interpretation to the God of the Bible. Lesbian sexuality did not feel unnatural. It occurred to me that I don't have to feel it to believe it. And then this opened up the Scriptures in a whole new way. My feelings fell with the fall. There is no shame in this.

I also was starting to learn something else: my struggle with any sin could be done to the glory of God, as repentance gives God glory. When God revealed himself to me, he left me with a driving, somewhat oxymoronic desire to make biblical sense of my place in the world as a woman covered by God. Although I had railed against normative gender roles for as long as I can remember, in both my heterosexual and homosexual relationships, I suddenly wanted to know what it would be like to be covered not only by God, but also to live under the protection of a godly husband. My conversion left me with a new sense of what sexuality is: a point of view where I could so love and treasure other image bearers that I sacrificed my lust for their purity, and one where, someday, even perhaps a woman like me could become the godly wife to a godly husband.

This was a spiritual awakening that opened me up to Scripture and to the Lord himself in a startling new way. My feelings were not proof that I didn't measure up. My journey into repentance was proof that I was one of God's own, one of the lost sheep, and he was leading me and guiding me and protecting me and comforting me.

I learned in this crucible to carefully distinguish common grace (which explains why my unbelieving friends are sometimes nicer, kinder, and more compassionate than my believing ones) from the fruit that grows from a redeemed life. Common grace is powerful, and I'm thankful for it, but it in itself is not a sign of Christian fruit. Christian fruit is known by its root (Christ), not by the contribution it makes to a better world. There is common grace that comes from common virtues, but only Christ can bear in someone fruit of saving grace. "All my springs of joy are in you," declares the last line of Psalm 87. God does not patch us up, putting bandages on those ruptured virtues we possess either from personality or from intelligence. No. God gives us a new passageway to his spring, out of which his living waters flow into us, and through which we have union with Christ.

Psalm 66:18 puts it this way: "If I had cherished iniquity in my heart, the Lord would not have listened" (ESV). We all have iniquity in our hearts, and we desperately need the Lord to listen. But when we cherish something that he does not, he will not listen. In the eighth chapter of the Bible, God says this: "The intent of man's heart is evil from his youth" (Gen. 8:21). Psalm 66 tells us not to cherish this evil intent of the heart. But who can ditch her own heart?

Apart from Christ, we can't stand against our own hearts.

Apart from Christ, we cannot stand against our own hearts. The verses above presume that we will struggle with sin, but they warn us not to declare any sin a "sanctifiable" character quality, even if through it we may learn valuable lessons about life. Learning lessons is not God's first priority for his children. Transformed character is. I learned here that God may, in his providence, bring good from my past, but the good that comes is not because of the sin, but in spite of it. It is very tempting to see "good" in those things that tempt us to sin or lead us to sin because then we don't seem nearly as corrupt as Original Sin renders us. According to God, sinful temptations are inclinations to do something or become something that cost Jesus his life for my sake. We are not to try to ransom it on our own terms. Suggesting that our sin is good or produces good is tantamount to calling cancer good health.

The verse in Genesis 8 shows that our hearts are not only sinful in the affections that we embrace, but even in the intent of those desires. As Hebrews 4:12 tells us, Scripture truly pierces the heart:

> For the word of God is living and active and sharper than any two-edged sword, and piercing as far as the division of soul and spirit, of both joints and marrow, and able to judge the thoughts and intentions of the heart.

It is a dangerous move to square off against Scripture, the

piercing Word that discerns and purifies. But how do I know if I am cherishing sin?

When we defend our right to a particular sin, when we claim it as an "I am," or a defining character trait, we are cherishing it, and separating ourselves from the God who promises rest for our soul through repentance and forgiveness. Jesus met sinners at the table. He sat at the table with them. But he did not join them in their choice sins. He sat with them, but he did not sin with them. We ought not expect Jesus to sin with us today. Isaiah 59:1–2 declares this: "Behold, the LORD's hand is not so short that it cannot save; nor is His ear so dull that it cannot hear. But your iniquities have made a separation between you and your God." When we cherish sin, we build a wall between our Maker and us. When we cherish sin we are asking God to overlook sin on the world's terms and not because of the blood of Christ.

When I lived as a lesbian, I truly believed that I was a better person for my lesbianism, my marginalized social status, my extended lesbian community and its commitment to social justice, and the egalitarianism of my lesbian relationships. I truly believed this. But after conversion, God showed me that if I was his, I could not ask him on my terms to rename something that he calls sin, because redemption cost him his blood. Every drop. If we believe that God uses sin as a creative way to bring wisdom and insight into the world, we are telling Jesus that his pain matters nothing to us. When we are owned by God, we are ruined for the world. And this marring of us for the world is one of the birthmarks of conversion.

Our feelings can—and often do—deceive us. When we believe that our sin is not really sin, we call God a liar, and we use our personal feelings as proof. All our personal feelings prove is that Original Sin and the deceptiveness of sin are inseparable.

But that still leaves the question unanswered: what is the sin of homosexuality? The sexual practice alone? The desire? What is temptation? Where do we draw the line between the temptation to sin and the sin itself?

Homosociality is an abiding and deep comfort afforded in keeping company with your own gender, and finding within your own gender your most important and cherished friendships. This is not a sin. Neither is this "gay." But once that comfort level shifts to sexually desiring a person with whom you are not biblically married, you are in sin. Since we have a sin nature, the question is not what to do *if* you sin (because you will). The question is what to do *when* you sin. How can we learn to enlist the Lord's power in defeating temptation before it defeats us?

But even if you see in yourself a temptation pattern, this does not mean that you are a dangerous person, unable to ever get close to people. This means for you what it means for me: that we are all good company when Jesus mediates our relationships. So yes, depending on what you do with them, feelings may be sinful. Jesus addresses this when he says: "Out of the heart come evil thoughts, murders, adulteries, fornications, thefts, false witness, slanders. These are the things which defile the man" (Matt. 15:19–20). I came away from this pivotal moment with this: homosexual lust is a sin, but so is heterosexual lust and *homophobia*. It is sinful to write people off because they sin in ways that offend you. God holds up the same mirror for us all, and none of us reflects the image of God in righteousness, holiness, and knowledge apart from Christ.

> Homophobia—the fear and hatred of people who identify as LGBT, and the wholesale writing off of their souls.

Sin must be fought at its deepest level. The root of my lesbianism was pride. The root of my heterosexual sin was pride as well. For others, the root of sexual sin may be lust or sexual addiction. Some sins are harder to battle than others. But God gives believers the gift of repentance. Repentance is a gift from God. And repentance is the daily posture of the Christian, not some one-time Sinner's Prayer shibboleth. We must never repent of sin in surface ways, like weeding our gardens by snipping the tops off of the dandelions. When we do this, we deceive ourselves and we risk hardening our heart to God's kind call. For it is the "kindness of God" that leads us to repentance (Rom. 2:4).

For my readers who lose the struggle with temptation and fall into sexual sin, please know that I (and other Christians) understand the shame and the temptation to hide your sin. Please, to the Christians who are reading this and do not struggle with homosexual desires, do not add weight to the burden by thinking that homosexuality is the biggest of all sins, or that its solution is heterosexuality. The solution to all sin is Christ's atoning blood. In Christ, we are new creatures. We are redeemed men and women who

Atonement—the reconciliation of God and humankind through Jesus Christ.

"have been buried with [Christ] through baptism into death" (Rom. 6:4) and are no longer slaves to the sin that once defined us, although likely it still knows our names. We are all called to holiness. And holiness violates my self-love and my confidence in my natural virtues. The Bible calls my natural virtues filthy garments: "For all of us have become like one who is unclean, and all our righteous deeds are like a filthy garment; and all of us wither like a leaf and our iniquities, like the wind, take us away" (Isa. 64:6). God repeats "all of us" three times. Not just some of us. All of us are in this snare if we trust in our natural virtues.

At the writing of this chapter, I am a fifty-two-year-old pastor's wife who homeschools two of her four children, serves the church where my husband, Kent, is the pastor, and tries to live as an "out" Christian. Kent and I got married on May 19, 2001, the day after he graduated from seminary. God has blessed us, and our marriage, faith, and family are places where we take true rest. But no matter how many years tick away, I am and will always be Rahab—a woman with a past. So, what does a person like me do with such a past? I have not forgotten. Body memories know my name. Details intrude into my world unpredictably, like when I am kneading the communion bread or homeschooling my children. I take each ancient token to the cross, for prayer, for more repentance, for thanksgiving that God is always right about matters of sin and grace. I think about what it means to inhabit the story of the Bible, and how repentance is a daily fruit of my new life in Christ. Paul's question in Romans 6:21 is one that I ask myself: "What fruit did you have then in the things of which you are now ashamed?" (NKJV).

The layers of my life in Christ always unfold in a double-directional way. I live and think in a forward way, preparing for eternity. But I continue to repent of sins I committed years ago, as the Lord brings them to mind from out of the miry depth of my history. I have come to understand that this soul business keeps me close to the Lord who is the keeper of my soul, my history, and my future.

I am told that stories like mine are dangerous. Conversions like mine have the potential to create "the danger of the single story," or the belief that converted people are changed. Both are true. Conversion stories are dangerous and converted people are changed by God. Converted people change and depart from their sins. We are all changed by justifying faith and the sanctification that God provides. We all repent and believe as a response to the Holy Spirit's gift of a new heart. We all stand with the blood of our Savior on our hands. That is the Bible's story. All who have met the risen Lord are changed. And we are all called to forsake the sin that we loved best before we met the Lord.

The Bible is inerrant, but my testimony is not. The testimony of who I was when God broke into my world is not diagnostic or proscriptic. But I leave it with you for your consideration and the reminder that Christ redeems your struggle by giving you greater union with him as you walk through it. Christ also gives you a new identity, the identity of one who overcomes.[2]

Identity

The Flame of Our Union in Christ

I know that I am not the only woman who feels out of place in church culture. Maybe it is my Myers-Briggs score: INTJ. (I am told that only one to three percent of the female population shares this score.) Or maybe it is the fact that I am a marked woman. Rahab. Mary Magdalene. Rosaria. Maybe it is that I am much more at home in the world of systematic theology or critical theory than in the strange and scary terrain of wedding or baby showers. And often I long for just one person in church to understand me.

My past as a lesbian puts any number of well-meaning churchy women into a total tailspin.

I recall once chopping vegetables in a lovely country kitchen for a Lord's Day fellowship meal. Sunlight was piping in through the curtains, and I was starting to feel at home in my new life as a married Christian woman. Another woman was in the kitchen assembling chicken and tomato sauce in a slow cooker. It was just she and I.

I enjoy the company of women, especially when we can be silent together, working in parallel worlds to build something. I have never felt the need to fill the peace of silence with empty chatter. She broke the silence with this question: "Is this safe? Being alone together in the kitchen?"

The question roused me out of my silence, at the same time that it baffled me. Kitchens—like libraries—are my safe spaces. *What could be unsafe here?*, I thought to myself. I must have had that dazed-dumb look on my face, because she repeated the question like this: "Does being alone with a woman bring back feelings for you? *Those* kind of feelings."

Suddenly, the danger was exposed: I.

It was I.

I was the potential source of unsafety.

I felt that chill of isolation creep in.

She couldn't even name *those* feelings, they were so dirty, or foreign, or dangerous.

I wanted to flee. I mumbled something about my being completely harmless, really, perhaps like an aged, neutered, and declawed cat, all the while wanting to say this: "Sister, don't flatter yourself."

I know.

Private fantasies of self-defense are unbecoming in a pastor's wife.

I was perplexed that even though I was a new creature in Christ, that was not good enough. I pondered why my identity in Christ did not seem to be good enough for her, and it made me wonder, again, if it was good enough for God. And I was puzzled, as I have never felt that Christians who have or had unasked-for homosexual desires are unsafe simply on the grounds of these unasked-for feelings.

And I have known *a lot* of people who fall into this camp.

Why did she not see that my identity in Christ was bigger than my past? Because there is another category of personhood that takes preeminence: sexual orientation. I will share the problems with this category in chapters 4 and 5, but for now I want to return to this painful moment. I share this anecdote to reveal that personal experience matters. I daily long to be understood and represented justly. And although I am a new creature in Christ, my past, although covered by Christ's blood, abides in a big way for some people. Identity in Christ, for me, always involves a healthy dose of war. War against the ghosts of who I once was, and war against the covetous machine of my own false entitlements.

In my church community, I want to do life together, sharing the joys and the ho-hums, and serving as general good company for the suffering. In order to have real community, we need to tell each other the stories of our lives. And we need to listen, even when someone else's story makes us uncomfortable. For this reason, in part, I wrote *Secret Thoughts*: I want you to know from what country I emigrated, and in which country my citizenship permanently and eternally resides. I'm not a native speaker of this country. No real convert is. I will always speak in broken godliness, as new paradigms reread old feelings.

Music forms the backdrop of my rumination, and I think of the role of my past as *obbligato*—accompanied with harmony, and not to be omitted. Therefore, for me and for you, life experience matters. It cannot and must not be dismissed. We who claim union with Christ and a personal relationship with him have experiential knowledge of our Maker and Redeemer, and this shapes what it means to have fellowship with other believers.

The question is, How does experience matter?

The question, then, is not whether experience matters—because it does. The question is, How does experience matter? Does personal experience serve as a form of truth? Can you trust your feelings? We become proficient at what we practice. This is true for obedience and for sin. What relationship does personal experience have with other frames of interpretation or worldview (including the Bible)? What responsibility do we have to others when we tell our stories?

Many barriers arise and prevent us from seeing ourselves clearly. Pastor Ken Smith believes that a big barrier to self-knowledge is that we fail to ask the right questions and then we fail to use the Bible to answer them. Ken's four questions about personhood are these: 1) Who am I? 2) What am I like? 3) What do I need? and 4) Where am I going? Let's explore the first three of Pastor Ken's questions in this chapter to help explain why identity in Christ matters.

Personal Identity in Christ's Historical Work: Who Am I?

Personal experience and personal suffering matter to Christ. Personal suffering, including the suffering that goes with recognizing my sin as sin, has a way of blinding me. In these moments, I find the words of the Puritan Elias Pledger to be a great comfort: "I will lay the weight of my sinking spirit on the free grace of Christ."[1] They tell me that, even as I wrestle with my sin, I need to cling more to Christ than to my feelings. And the only way to do this is to invest in the attributes of God, the suffering of Christ, and the comfort of the Holy Spirit. If I create an identity carved out of my personal pain, even one caused by the sins of my flesh, I will forever struggle in a separate sphere from my God. For that reason, I believe that my personal experience must always be surrendered to what my triune God has done and who my triune God is.

My personal experience must be surrendered because it cannot reach back to God's eternal and transient history. Our scope and scale is too limited. I cannot find my identity in what I have done. I can only find my identity in what God has done and is doing.

God set apart a people from the foundation of the world. In that way, God's people—all who will believe in and call upon Christ alone for salvation—were elected from all eternity. Ephesians 1:4 declares this: "He chose us in Him before the foundation of the world, that we would be holy and blameless before Him." From the foundation of the world is a very long time. It reveals God's forbearance and his patience, as well as his special knowledge of his children, that he did not destroy us as soon as we were born. Because of God's eternal purpose in Christ, salvation needed to come to pass.

God redeemed his people through the blood of Christ, baptizing believers through his death and resurrection. We learn this in Romans 6:

> *3 Or do you not know that all of us **who have been baptized** into Christ Jesus have been baptized into His **death**?*
> *4 Therefore we **have been buried** with Him through baptism into **death**, so that as Christ was raised from the dead through the glory of the Father, so we too might walk in newness of life.*

*5 For if we have **become united** with Him in the likeness of His **death**, certainly we **shall also be** in the likeness of His resurrection,*

*6 knowing this, that our **old self was crucified** with Him, in order that our body of sin might be done away with, so that we would no longer be slaves to sin;*

*7 for he who has **died** is freed from sin.*

*8 Now if we have **died** with Christ, we believe that we shall also **live** with Him,*

9 knowing that Christ, having been raised from the dead, is never to die again; death no longer is master over Him.

10 For the death that He died, He died to sin once for all; but the life that He lives, He lives to God.

11 Even so, consider yourselves to be dead to sin but alive to God in Christ Jesus. [emphasis added]

Each line paints a stark contrast between the binary opposites of death and life. This word-picture of water baptism highlights the spiritual realities of what union with Christ means. Each line calls me to move my heart, feet, and hands, and to do this today. We can only trust this hope because Jesus embodies truth. Ideas such as "have been baptized into," "have been buried with," and "have become united to" use a special verb tense called present perfect progressive. This verb tense is used to communicate that Christ's work is finished (or "perfect"). While it was finished before we were physically born, because believers were set apart before the foundations of the world, we are living out today (present) the fruits of Christ's work.

Finally, the use of the helping verb "have" included in these phrases makes the verb something we call perfect progressive: that is, Christ's work is perfect (finished) and progressive (living on, albeit imperfectly, in his redeemed people). Here we see that our identity in Christ is transient: we are who we are not only because of who we are today, but because of the meaning of Christ's *mediatorial* death and resurrection in us. Thus, our personal experience

Mediatorial—relating to a mediator or go-between.

with God has a history that precedes our consciousness. Just as our physical parents likely have memories of us that precede our own, so too God our Father remembers us from before the world's beginnings.

The life story that I share in chapter 1 does not reveal the fullness of God's perfect plan. It does not show the future glory God holds. And it does not show the history wrecked by the fall of humanity, which scarred us all through Original Sin.

Identity tells me who I am. And, consequently, identity tells me who I am not.

Union with Christ is part of the saints' armor.

One more crucial gift that identity in Christ bequeaths is it gives me a way to defend myself against Satan's accusations. Union with Christ is part of the saints' armor. Satan is the father of lies and the great deceiver whose crafty seductions initiated Adam's fall. When he attacks, he holds an ancient claim on me. Satan lures you into sin by suggesting that it is no big deal, that its consequence is not deadly. Hence his first question to Eve: "Did God really say?" But once you have sinned, Satan accuses you with the full wrath of God, a wrath that he knows particularly well and that he wants believers to falsely own as well. Satan uses the sin of my past and the sin of my present life as extortion. He daily tells me that if my sin was revealed in its totality, everyone would know I'm a fake, a condemned sinner. In my ear, Satan hisses, "I know who you are, and I know what you have done." And Satan is right in a half-truth kind of way. He is right when he says that I have sinned grievously. And he is right when he says that God judges sin and that my sin deserves death. Satan knows Romans 3:23 also: "for all have sinned and fall short of the glory of God."

But my identity is in the risen Christ, not in some moralistic notion that I am all cleaned up or some flimsy theology that says I only needed to repent in some general sweep when I "accepted" Christ. Because my identity is in Christ, like Christian in *Pilgrim's Progress*, I have to set the record straight and what fuels my resolve is deep and daily repentance to God. To my accuser I say: "You are right about the depths of my sin. You are more right than you know. I am guilty of that and so much more. And you are right that God's punishment for what I have done is death. But here is what you do not know. You don't seem to know Romans 6:3–11. Do you know what this passage means? Because of my union with Christ, I was put on trial. I was taken into custody. I was spat on and stripped naked. I was thrashed with metal whips by Pontius Pilate. I was tortured. I was crucified. I was castigated to hell.

"And every time I embrace the means of grace, every time I read the Word of God and it convicts me of my sin, and every time I respond to God's wisdom in repentance and confession of sin, every time I worship God and eat his body and drink his blood, I am risen from the tomb and resurrected into the light by the power of Jesus Christ himself, who declares to me that there is no condemnation for me any longer, because I am clothed in his righteousness by the power of his resurrection. The risen Christ in whom I stand declares to you, Satan, that you no longer have any claim on me."

I have to have this conversation with Satan every day.

For that reason, my identity in Christ cannot be rented by sentimental attachments. It must be owned and sealed with blood.

Personal Identity and the Fall: What Am I Like?

My personal history, according to Ephesians 1, did not start with my conscious understanding of who I am or what I am like. My personal history started from "before the foundations of the world." But things got topsy-turvy in the garden of Eden. Although I wasn't present in body, because Adam is my *federal head*, it is back to the garden that we must go to see what I am like, and why personal identity is not of my own doing and not of my own definition.

Federal head — someone who acts on behalf of others as part of an agreement or treaty.

Adam's first sin did not merely set a bad example or hold theological significance because it was a mere sin of origin — something that established the wrong musical key or held

41

theological significance because it set the stage for bad choice-making starting at the moment of our birth.[2] Sin is more complex and seductive than that. Sin has agency and intent. It is alive, and it is an active force in the spiritual warfare of a believer. Adam's first sin is called Original Sin, and it imparts the reality that my consciousness fell thousands of years ago, long before my first birthday.

This means something that sounds unjust: I am not a sinner because I sin. Rather, I sin because I am a sinner, born with a sin nature because Adam represented me in Eden (Rom. 5:12–14). We are guilty from conception (Ps. 51:5), and wholly inclined to evil (Eph. 2:1–3). Our guilt is *coram Deo*—before the face of God— and not merely as a breach in human relationships. Through Adam, we inherit what is called the twofold problem of sin: guilt and corruption.[3] Truth be told, this feels immeasurably unfair. But as we assess this feeling of unfairness, we need to remember that God graciously provides a better way forward in Christ than we would have had in Adam. Standing in the line of Adam is a presupposition and a premise to the gospel. As Joel Beeke puts it, "To deny the fall of man into sin is to rob the death of Christ of its redemptive meaning and saving power."[4]

The term of the Reformers here—*total depravity*—resonates with me. Total depravity does not mean that we always do the very worst thing that we can do, or always sin in the biggest way possible, or that we are as bad as we can possibly be. Rather, it means that, because sin extends to every part of our body, being, and soul, we are totally unable to save ourselves from this predicament. Daily, we add to our inheritance in Adam by committing sins against God and our friends. It means that the best of our intentions fail us, and, even after conversion, indwelling sin holds the power of manipulation. Time and time again.

This is what I am like.

We cannot understand the ramifications of peace through the atoning blood of Jesus unless we first stop to ponder the way that Scripture describes anyone not in Christ's relationship to God: as enemies in an all-out war. Indeed, when God sent his only begotten Son to become sin on our behalf, God saved us from one thing: himself. We cannot soft-pedal this reality: God saves us from himself. Psalm 7 records the war: his bow is ready, and arrows will penetrate into the hearts of all impenitent sinners.

Because our only access to God is through the mediatorial work of Christ, won hard through the bloody and immeasurable suffering of Jesus (Rom. 3:9–18), God's fury is directed against every man, woman, and child who is not covered by that blood. Adding to this is Satan, roaming through the world like a roaring lion. First Peter 5:8 declares, "Be of sober spirit, be on the alert. Your adversary, the devil, prowls around like a roaring lion, seeking someone to devour." The threat of a roaming lion is frightening enough, but also ponder the following: lions roar after they have killed and for the intent of scaring their prey into running from cover. This tells me that Satan's threat comes with blood spilled and battles won. This is not a pretty picture. As Russell Moore puts it: "The canon of Scripture shows us tracks of blood from the very edge of Eden outward. The biblical story immediately veers from Paradise to depictions of murder, drunkenness, incest, gang rape, polygamy, and on and on and on, right down to whatever is happening with you."[5]

The question hangs heavily: what is happening with you (and with me)?

The term *sola scriptura* gives comfort to the believer, because through it we have access to our full history. If we go to a medical doctor and we do not have access to our personal medical history, the doctor may miss some lifesaving detail. I am a mother by adoption, and I think about this every time we are at the doctor. The first time that my daughter was put on penicillin, she was sixteen months old. After five

Sola scriptura — the Bible alone; the Bible's grand narrative framing my own.

hours it was obvious that she was developing a serious allergy. By God's grace, her allergic reaction was controllable, but it left me wondering: what other potentially lifesaving information does my daughter not have? As a mother by adoption, I learned of her penicillin allergy the hard way. More importantly, so did my daughter.

The same is true when we live our lives based on good intentions, good deeds, and well-meaning self-diagnoses. We, too, without accurate history from our lineage in Adam, come at things with a dangerous absence of information. Without the full history of Scripture, good intentions are not enough to accurately represent who we are and what we need. Our triune God is our enigmatic completion. The wisdom of the Bible is an alien wisdom, for without it we are clueless. Even after the Holy Spirit exchanges your stony heart for one that pumps veins fat with Christ's blood, and you can walk in a Bible-on-life and life-on-Bible path, the war is still on.

Sola experiencia—my personal experience framing and shaping and selecting those parts of the Bible that I judge relevant for me.

There is another term, though, that daily competes for my allegiance. It is *sola experiencia*. *Sola scriptura* puts the hand of the suffering into the hand of the Savior by asserting the priority of Scripture to govern personal experience. However, *sola experiencia* separates me from that God—the God who made me, takes care of me, providentially allows for my afflictions, comforts me as I seek to walk in obedience to him, and gives me victory, either by granting liberty from temptations, or granting humility over how dearly I need the Lord's forgiveness, kind company, and the renewal of hope through fellow Christians who love me and do life with me. Before I knew Christ, all I had was my personal experience and my best intentions on how to craft a life of decency in response to it. Conversion woke me to God's blinding interrogator's light, revealing that identity in Christ demands heroic sacrifices, sacrifices that can only be wrought by God's power and indwelling grace.

The Bible tells me that I have a longer history with God than my memory allows, and it takes me past the garden of Eden to a majestic place called "before the foundations of the world." This is the biblical story. This is the true story. But this may not be—and often is not—the real or experiential story of my deepest feelings. The real (the flesh-living fact of my life) and the true (God's story and his grace to me) disengaged in the garden, when all creation groaned because of the fall, and when sin entered the world and writhed seemingly undetected into the nature of all people. When the real (what I feel) and the true (what God declares) do not come together, we feel a stinging vestige of the fall, with the painful knowledge that choosing between ourselves and God is a hue of death, only imaginable through Christ's ransom.

When feelings are not translated through biblical wisdom, we become unmoored. We lose our anchor, and we wonder why God isn't giving us permission to act on our feelings. This is especially agonizing when our intuition lines up with our experiences. Christians often use the expression "God told me" to describe a wide range of personal, intuitive decisions. We all know that it is very hard to distinguish a call from God from a burning personal desire. And even though we are new creatures in Christ, we still have a heart condition. Jeremiah 17:9 diagnoses our heart condition like this: "The heart is more deceitful than all else and is desperately sick."

Our God is a personal God, and he does impress upon us— in intimate, loving, personal ways—his call on our lives, in all of its providential and sometimes heartbreaking details. This is why he gave us his Word. Proverbs 23:7 says, "For as he thinks within himself, so he is." We are what we think. Ultimately, our intuition of God's call on our lives must be arbitrated by the Word of God. As John Owen says, "The law grace writes in our hearts must answer to the law written in God's word."[6] In other words, God's grace does not grant permission to ramrod into sin because it feels good. Instead, grace answers to the law of God, found in Scripture, and not to the law of my own sin or personal desire.

God speaks to us through his Word manifested in our day-to-day lives. I started college as a music major, and one of my favorite classes was Ear Training and Sight Singing. There we learned to hear pitch and define it accurately, to read music and sing the note on the staff without musical accompaniment by recalling it to mind from the ear. We learned how to hear true music within our minds amid a world of silence or noise. We learned how to discern pitch and pathos no matter what else was going on. The same is true for Christians. We learn to discern the voice of God from the cacophony of the world and the seduction of the enemy.

Sadly, the voice of the enemy often uses our vulnerabilities and weaknesses to slay, rape, and pillage. Satan specializes in half-truths, in twisting the truth, and in appearing to redeem that which God calls sin. I often ponder those verses found in 1 Thessalonians 5: "Do not despise prophetic utterances. But examine everything carefully; hold fast to that which is good; abstain from every form of evil" (vv. 20-22). This passage reminds me that the exclusive claims of Christ will always have an edge; and I will meet that edge in the desires of my heart. In these verses, Paul gives us no liberty to hybridize gospel truth with the world's cares. Because the Bible manifests God's character of immutability, its wisdom—while composed before the world began—anticipates our need today, including equipping us with the wisdom we need to protect ourselves from Satan. "Did God really say?" was Satan's question to Eve. On face value, it seems simple enough.

> But nothing good comes of Satan. Nothing.

But nothing good comes of Satan. Nothing. Not even a question from Satan is innocent. The invitation to challenge God's authority calls out the covetous beast in us all. But often we don't even wait for Satan to ask before jumping into the pit. We long to sample a little of the world's flavors, to try out some of its delicacies and ideas, and to not have to feel like such a freak who can't stay apace with culture or popularity. Those COEXIST bumper stickers seem so wise at times, so friendly, so willing to meet people where they are. Sometimes we wonder: doesn't unity depend on seeing things from the point of view of the world? How else can we stand with the disempowered? What is so wrong with that?

Identity in Christ depends on vigilance on this point: God's point of view must become mine, no matter how foreign such a concept is, how impossible our situation appears, or how deformed an anomaly we become to our friends. Vigilance is an exhausting stance, to be sure, and I am grateful that Christ hangs on to me as I seek to apply those verses in 1 Thessalonians.

Satan's first attack on me is often in regards to my point of view—just as he attacked Christ on his point of view during the wilderness temptation (Luke 4). I have met Satan more than once in the last two years disguised as a brother or sister seeking Christian unity and peace, often twisting God's truth with heartfelt personal experience. Recently the pastor of a well-respected church asked me to meet with a woman who was part of his counseling staff. When I entered her office, she directed me to a comfortable chair and made one simple request: "Rosaria, I want you to change your message." I found this a bold and disarming request, and so I told her that I come in the gospel of peace.

She said, "Change your message."

I told her that I stand in the risen Christ.

She said, "Change your message."

Finally, I asked her what I ought to change in my message.

She said, "Tell people that it is only in your opinion that homosexual practice is a sin."

I responded by letting her know that I am not smart enough to have this opinion, but that this is the position the inspired and inerrant Word of God upholds. It comes to me from the historic Christian church, handed down to us from the Apostles' Creed, through the pages of Scripture, and so on down to me. I told her that changing my message would involve denying the plain meaning of Scripture, the testimony of the church, the life, death, and resurrection of Jesus, and the gospel.

But to the postmodern mind, this line of thinking is no slam dunk. From a postmodern perspective, her request seems reasonable enough: just own this position of mine as a personal point of view. But claiming something that is a universal truth to be a mere matter of personal preference is a lie by omission. This is the Bible's message, and apart from Christ, I am more condemned by it than the woman who made this request.

The question remains: is the Bible's message regulated by my personal experience (if the shoe fits, then wear it; if not, amend it to fit your experience)? Or is the Bible's message global? Are natural virtues good enough, or are we all, apart from Christ, unable to reflect God's expectations?

Christian unity cannot be crafted by abdicating or disguising the named identity that God gives to us. We are called to define ourselves in and through him alone. Unity depends on biblical truth, and all forms of evil must be shunned, even when its form dances in our consciousness as unwelcome but persistent company. These vestiges of the fall in our redeemed minds reveal that our imperfect sanctification will only find completion in glory. What else can we do but cling to Christ for continued renewal through the fruit of repentance, hungry for heaven?

God wants us to hear his voice through the Word of God, the discernment of the Holy Spirit, and the comfort of our redeemed life through the blood of Christ. For example, musical pitch is black and white. It is accurate, sharp, or flat. It cannot be both accurate and flat. It is exclusive in its claims. While a chorus can sing in harmony or cacophony (dissonance), a solo voice can only be accurate, sharp, or flat. So too is Scripture. And even though words have what linguists call a semantic range of meaning[7] (and I will discuss this later in the book when I talk about the use of the term "gay Christian"), let us be very clear that while words can be both used and misused, God expects us to find the bulls-eye when it comes to his Word and its meaning. That is, we can never explain away the plain meaning of Scripture or its historic testimony in the church by this. The Bible is a unified biblical revelation, and while it communicates through chosen men, because each was inspired by the Holy Spirit, it is God's unified voice. We train our ears to hear God by knowing deeply his direct Word and the theological principles that emerge from it.

I am not talking here about the themes of Christianity that we create in man-made hymns or personal artwork or dance. Nothing that we create will have the power to save, discern, or sanctify. Christian culture may be uplifting, but never at the expense of God's Word. Not one creation of ours will come close to the sharp edges and sanctifying blood of our Savior.[8] We commit our lives to the Jesus of the Bible, the Word made flesh who came to fulfill the whole law of God. Our personal experiences matter, as they all happen under the watchful providence of a merciful and loving God. But our personal experiences do not measure the validity of God's commands. We are not called to judge God, but rather to die to self. He is the potter, we are the clay. And our Savior stands inseparable from the Word: "He is clothed with a robe dripped in blood, and His name is called The Word of God" (Rev. 19:13).

Personal Identity through Union with Christ: What Do I Need? (Part 1)

Union with Christ is a concept that helps explain the depths and width of how the believer finds life only "through God in Christ." Colossians 3:3 says, "For you have died and your life is hidden with Christ in God." Reformed theologians teach that believers have union with Christ in three interdependent ways:[9]

1) *immanent union*—having union with Christ from all eternity, as God set apart a people for himself from before the foundations of the world (Eph. 1:4);

2) *transient union*—having union with Christ in his death and resurrection, and having our identity born of this (Rom. 6:3–11);

3) *applicatory union*—the present and ongoing lived application of how Christ indwells us and directs us today and forevermore (Eph. 2:5–7).[10]

Our union with Christ is through grace until glory. When we realize that union with Christ is foundational, historical, ontological, eternal, and remaining, we are more likely to surrender ourselves to be conformed to Christ's image, and less likely to render Jesus our imaginary friend who kindly condones all that we want because we believe in him.

Union with Christ helps us to work through the limits of (present-day) personal experience. It helps me understand something important about my own conversion. It helps me rethink that Lord's Day afternoon in that country kitchen when I was—for the hundreth time—misunderstood by someone who was supposed to see me as a sister in the Lord.

When the Lord entered my world, I experienced that gospel-ignited "expulsive power of a new affection" (to quote the title of Thomas Chalmers's famous sermon). That new affection was not heterosexuality, but Jesus, my Jesus, my friend and Savior. I was not converted out of homosexuality. I was converted out of unbelief. After my life in Jesus unfolded through conversion and the means of grace that God gives to his people (Bible reading, prayer, church membership, taking of the sacraments), I realized that my sin was not exclusively a sexual desire for women. My sexual desire for women hinged upon another sin. It danced on the glittering tip of the knife of pride. I was dealing with a pride that rejected patriarchy as a flat-out danger and, combining this with a homosocial affinity to women that neatly morphed into sexual practice, it was easy to claim myself a lesbian.

> I became that which I had formerly loathed.

When God saved me, the renewing of my mind made me feel like I was losing my mind. Everything in my life changed. Everything. Upon conversion, the fact that women were sexually off-limits was clear, and while my body memories still claimed my attention, these winnowed, and God gave me peace through my union with Christ. While throbbing and formidable, my identity crisis necessitated my identity in Christ. I became that which I had formerly loathed and laughed at. Eventually, God gave a deep and genuine (and somewhat ironic) desire to be a godly wife, if the Lord willed.

Sexuality in our fallen and even redeemed bodies travels on a complex continuum. God knows that (and that is why he is jealous for a sexuality that corresponds to his creation order, including a sexuality of sacrificial celibacy). When the gospel meets a sexual identity and practice apart from God's intended order in the life of one of his sheep, Jesus places a yoke of love upon you, and while the burden of loss of who you once were does not feel light, as Jesus carries the heavier part of this cross, it is good. This is how I first experienced union with Christ. It made me realize that "it is good for me that I was afflicted, that I [might] learn Your statutes" (Ps. 119:71). The opening clause of this verse, "it is good," is a hard one. It reveals that when you are in union with Christ, God blesses you through affliction, so that you may learn obedience. Even Jesus learned obedience through suffering (Heb. 5).

Union with Christ and identity in Christ conjoin because we are made in the image of God. But where does God's image reside in men and women? John Calvin (1509–1564) situates God's image primarily in the soul of men and women, as this is the feature that distinguishes humanity from all other creation.

While the soul is God's fingerprint on humanity, the body too will be resurrected. The Westminster Divines point out that humanity "in the totality of… physical-spiritual being is (rather than merely contains) the image of God."[11] Before *the fall*, Adam and Eve bore God's image in true "knowledge, righteousness, and holiness."[12] And although frightfully deformed, the image of God still remains in humanity after the fall as well. Calvin maintained that the fall did not merely mean that humanity lost a likeness of God. The fall was more than a crack in the facade. After the fall, man's reason and will were both distorted and perverted.

The fall—The fall is the event in the garden of Eden where Adam and Eve disobeyed God and ate of The Tree of the Knowledge of Good and Evil (Gen. 2–3).

The first chapter of Genesis reveals creation before the fall: "God created man in His own image, in the image of God He created him; male and female, He created them" (v. 27). This tells us that both men and women are created in God's image. Even now as fallen creatures, we were created in God's image.

But after we are called by God, redeemed by Christ, and renewed by the Holy Spirit, God commands us to "put on the new self" (Col. 3:10). Ephesians 4:24 commands us to "put on the new self, which in the likeness of God has been created in righteousness and holiness of the truth." This command is fleshed out more thoroughly in the surrounding verses:

> *22 in reference to your former manner of life, you lay aside the old self, which is being corrupted in accordance with the lusts of deceit,*
> *23 and that you be renewed in the spirit of your mind,*
> *24 and put on the new self, which in the likeness of God, has been created in righteousness and holiness of the truth.*
> *25 Therefore, laying aside falsehood, speak truth each one of you with his neighbor, for we are members of one another.*

These commands and promises reveal the equity with which God sets apart his people. These verses also show that there is always a gospel road into someone's life because sin is the great leveler, formulating the comprehensive democratic condition of us all.

Personal Identity through Sanctification: What Do I Need? (Part 2)

Salvation is a great gift and mystery. God justifies the sinner through Christ's atoning blood. He grants us the gift of faith. The power to believe comes from God, but the act is still our own. Christ infuses (or pours in) his hard-won renewal of life. Where, then, does salvation begin? It begins with God the Father's election, his justifying love, and his legal pardon. Justification is an act of God's free grace. God's offer of pardon demands a response. When God calls a sinner to himself, we commit our lives to Jesus, the author and finisher of our faith (Heb. 12:2). Then we begin the lifelong journey of sanctification, being set apart and being made holy. Only Christ's atoning blood meets God's requirement of justice, and this is why,

Justification— the action of God declaring me righteous in his sight.

Sanctification—the process of my becoming more like Jesus.

no matter how hard I try, I cannot save myself. When the Holy Spirit gives a person a new heart, the blood of our Savior renews the whole person "in the image of God."[13] The metaphor that the New Testament gives for this is death and resurrection, or dying unto sin and living unto newness of life. But what exactly does this renewal in the whole person mean?

Romans 6:6 reveals that sanctification equips the believer to go into the battle against sin, reminding us that "our old self was crucified with him, in order that our body of sin might be done away with, so that we would no longer be slaves to sin." The promise here is not that we are given total liberty over sin, but that we are works in process. This process of subduing sin and having victory over it is described in the context of a battle (Rom. 8:13). Battles take time, bloodshed, and courage. This tells us that sanctification is a process, and it sometimes feels slow and circular. But if you are justified by God, you *are* in the process of being sanctified.

In a practical way, this means that while you may still have sinful desires, God equips you to not act on them. If you, by temperament and practice, have a problem with the sin of anger, God will give to you through his gift of sanctification (as you respond in love by applying yourself to the means of grace) the ability to control yourself. This does not mean that you will necessarily have a cessation of anger or angry feelings, but rather, you will have the ability to react differently as they emerge. As the Westminster Divines put it, in sanctification, sin is subdued, but not necessarily eradicated until glory.

We also see in Scripture that sanctification is not equal in all believers. Some people are given greater mastery over sin than others. First John 2 says,

> 12 I am writing to you, little children, because your sins have been forgiven you for His name's sake.
> 13 I am writing to you, fathers, because you know Him who has been from the beginning. I am writing to you, young men, because you have overcome the evil one. I have written to you, children, because you know the Father.

14 I have written to you, fathers, because you know Him who has been from the beginning. I have written to you, young men, because you are strong, and the word of God abides in you, and you have overcome the evil one.

These verses reveal and give glory to God for different measures of sanctifying grace in the different believers mentioned here: little children, fathers, older children, young men. These categories refer not to literal age, but spiritual age: new believers to tested-and-tried believers. This passage reveals that God gives you your portion, and that we can trust that those whom God justifies, he also sanctifies and will one day glorify. We strive to work with God in sanctification by calling sin "sin" and by giving him our heart, but we do not strive against God by demanding perfection of ourselves or others. Through sanctification, God "[trains our senses] to discern good and evil" (Heb. 5:14).

Sanctification is not perfect or complete in any Christian in this lifetime, and this is not a sign that the believer is failing to do something (although we do need to keep ourselves in check and make sure that we are applying the means of grace in our lives). It is tempting to fall into the error of seeing sanctification as something that we do, and not a work of God in us to which we respond in love and humility. The Bible gives us one reason why sanctification is imperfect and unequal: our sinful nature, even after we are born again, lives on in us. Hebrews 12:1 commands us to run, even while acknowledging that we do so with the potential for entangling sin: "Therefore, since we have so great a cloud of witnesses surrounding us, let us also lay aside every encumbrance and the sin which so easily entangles us, and let us run with endurance the race that is set before us." We often feel crippled by sin. But disabled or crippled, God still calls us—and equips us—to run.

I often speak to people who believe that God is not hearing their prayer because they have prayed their whole lives for God to take away the particular sin of unwanted homosexual desire, and he has not. I will address this specific issue more in the next chapter, when we look at the three kinds of sin believers must battle daily: original, actual, and indwelling. But for now, we need to remember that sanctification puts a wedge between you and your sin, and dislodges your allegiance to sin, but temptations may well live long. Temptation patterns linger, but they do not rule your life anymore and they do not define you. Temptation patterns are outsiders to your true nature in Christ. They don't co-reign with Christ even as they remain. But if you are alive, you struggle with temptation. And if you have become an expert in practicing a particular sin, you can bet your bottom dollar that you have body memories that can recall this well-practiced sin to mind. I sure do. It is crucial for those of us with long track records of cultivating indwelling sin to know our enemy: woe to you if you grow sentimental about these loitering temptation patterns and try to make just a little room for them in your life.

Sometimes when I speak to church and college audiences, I am asked if I am healed. Sometimes the person asking the question will say: "God does not make people gay. So if your homosexual desire does not disappear in this lifetime, then you are either not a believer or not praying hard enough." Both the use of the term "healing" and the "pray the gay away" philosophy strike an unbiblical chord to me, and I said that to my questioner.

In my life, I have experienced how the Lord has both forgiven my sin and delivered me from it, but that does not mean that temptations do not tarry. Sin is sin.

Sin is treason, not sinus trouble.

Sin is treason, not sinus trouble. God forgives sin; he does not heal sin. Indeed, there is something deeply deceptive about praying that God would give me only what I need to be strong in myself. The strength that the gospel promises is the strength found only in continued dependence upon Christ. We know from the Bible that not until glory will we experience full sanctification and the complete eradication of our sinful nature. But do not let this minimize your hope for vitality in Christ today. Today is the day of salvation and sanctification, for you and for me. Like Jacob, we must lay hold of God and not let go (Gen. 32:24–32).

One reason I am writing this book is that I believe we need a more stalwart understanding of sin, repentance, and sanctification to provide pastoral care to all people struggling with unwanted sexual temptations. We must stop seeing sin and sanctification exclusively as things that we do. Deliverance from a lifelong sin pattern means that you—with God's strength—have the ablity to not act on that which God forbids, and to not love that which God abhors. It also means that if you fall, through repentance, you are renewed, knowing that falling does not mean falling away. It means that you grow in humility, knowing that you need the Lord every step of the way. God gives you victory over sin, but he does not lobotomize you. God warns us to not put confidence in ourselves, but only in him: "let him who thinks he stands take heed that he does not fall" (1 Cor. 10:12). God gives victory by equipping you to do battle with sin, and by giving you the humility to know that you need him every step of the way. Since warriors can get battle weary, God calls us to walk alongside one another to extend kind comfort. James 5:16 comforts us with this: "Therefore, confess your sins to one another, and pray for one another so that you may be healed. The effective prayer of a righteous man can accomplish much."

We desire victory over sin because we desire to be ever close to God. "The nearness of God is my good," declares Psalm 73:28. I long to walk side-by-side with fellow believers who are in the battle. But Scripture warns us against the danger of denying our guilt, even when the sin with which we struggle is unasked for and unwanted. That is, Scripture warns us against pitting our point of view against God's: 1 John 1:8: says, "If we say that we have no sin, we are deceiving ourselves and the truth is not in us." This tells me that what I need is the ability to see my life from God's point of view. And when we have God's Spirit renewing us daily, we have real hope that the God who has forgiven our sin will also deliver us from temptation to sin. I have tasted this sweet gift, and the Lord freely gives this grace to those who seek him.

We also struggle with the reality that God dispenses sanctifying grace in different measures. It is very hard for

American Christians to see that God gives some people one cross to bear and others ten. Indeed, this violates our sense of fairness and justice. But we don't get to choose the portion that God gives to us. And it is not Christian kindness to deny to fellow image bearers that following Christ is hard and will cost you everything. Philippians 3 powerfully reveals Paul's ongoing struggle with sin:

> 12 Not that I have already obtained it or have already become perfect, but I press on so that I may lay hold of that for which also I was laid hold of by Christ Jesus.
> 13 Brethren, I do not regard myself as having laid hold of it yet; but one thing I do: forgetting what lies behind and reaching forward to what lies ahead;
> 14 I press on toward the goal for the prize of the upward call of God in Christ Jesus.

Like Paul, we are called to press on in God's strength and continue our battle against sin. We can trust God that he knows what sin is. And if we are a believer, having been justified by God, we are called to respond to God's gift with daily renewed love for God and his means of grace.

Through salvation, God gets the glory, while we who are saved and being sanctified, get the blessing.

If we rush through Bible reading and prayer time, we miss the blessing and the power. Often because of misplaced priorities, we unwittingly limp along on a starvation diet of Scripture, forgetting that we have an appointment with Satan, our deceiver and accuser, the minute we rise from our reading chair. Our time in the Word and in prayer should change us. Through it, we should be transformed, equipped, encouraged, and prepared. We should never neglect our Bible reading and prayer time, knowing that we do so only at our own spiritual peril.

But if we get the blessing, why do we sometimes struggle with shame? Why is it hard to remember who we are in Christ?

Shame is my biggest nightmare, and I imagine that if you also come to Christ out of a life of sexual sin, you might feel the same way. Shame is what we feel when Romans 2:14–16 hits home, knowing deep down and without a doubt that God will judge the secrets of men.

Repentance

The Threshold to God and the Answer to Shame, Temptation, and Sin

Shame.

No one likes the feeling of shame. No one likes to be shamed. If you do a quick word search on shame, you will see that its English roots take us directly to exposure and sexuality. Shame is the self-loathing, gut response to getting caught and knowing that God has the right and responsibility to judge (Rom. 2:14–16). Tellingly, Adam and Eve's first emotional response to their sin was shame, and they sought to deal with their shame by hiding from God and covering their bodies. When our evil is exposed, we do the same thing: duck and cover.

When Christ claimed me for his own and I responded in surrender, I thought that shame would be a distant memory. I thought that being a new creature in Christ would insulate me against the shame of my life, from the blasphemy of my atheism (and teaching thousands of students from this perspective), to the heterosexual and homosexual sin I had committed, and in the false pride of my people-pleasing.

But something wasn't working the way I imagined the Christian life was supposed to work. Instead of feeling cleansed by the blood of Christ, I felt shamed by it. Under the lens of my Savior's life, death, and love, I realized that only a holy God could forgive me. I understood that no mortal man could forgive my sin. But somehow and for some reason, I kept doubting the love of God. In fact, one problem with shame was that it just wouldn't stay in my past. The more that I read the Bible, the more sin that God uncovered in my present life. And it seemed to me that the sin I was presently committing—as a believer—was far more heinous than anything I did before I knew the risen Christ.

A friend in the Syracuse church tried to help me with this. She gave me the book *Tired of Trying to Measure Up* by Jeff VanVonderen.[1] I read the whole book in one sitting (as I tend to do with books). I cheered all the way through Part 1, whose overarching theme is how shame wounds people, and how these wounds compel us to work harder at measuring up to the standard other people set for us. Part 1 had Rosaria written on every page. I'm a workaholic. I would have made a great Pharisee, if only sexual sin hadn't taken me captive. I am deeply self-righteous. Pride is my raging and most dearly developed character trait. Like Sisyphus—the Greek mythological king whose punishment for chronic deceitfulness involved rolling an enormous boulder up a hill, watching it roll down, and then performing this perpetual ineffective motion for eternity—I can never run hard enough or fast enough to best the burden that dogs me.

But then I got to Part 2 of this book, and I stopped tracking with it. The overarching theme of Part 2 is that when shame wounds people, grace heals them. How? By remembering that we committed our life to Christ and by claiming and choosing to stand in the Spirit. What's wrong with this? you might ask. How can anyone argue with grace? How can anyone argue with God's gift of the fruit of the Spirit after conversion? Something about seeing grace as the solution to shame didn't make sense to me. It felt to me like a step was missing. I would later learn that the missing step was repentance, and that this could be for someone a deadly step to miss.

My problem was that Psalm 119 kept ringing in my ears. The psalm starts out with foregrounding David's problem with shame. He cries, "Oh, that my ways may be established to keep your statutes! Then I shall not be ashamed when I look upon all your commandments" (vv. 5–6). Here, David turns to the law to sort out his shame. It is not that he couldn't have asked for grace. The Psalms are replete with cries for grace, mercy, and SOS calls for help in times of dire need. But David begs for the law to be effective in breaking down the strongholds of sin. David says here that he will be free of shame when he "looks upon all [of God's] commandments (all of God's moral law)." David knew that the law does not save, but he shows us something that VanVonderen misses about grace. Grace isn't like the lollipop the doctor gives my son to distract him from the flu shot. Grace doesn't make obedience negotiable. Grace is what picks me up out of the miry pit (Psalm 40) when the law, my tutor, condemns my natural sense of self-righteousness. When the law reveals my sin, God's grace compels me, fuels me, inspires me to repent, knowing that it is against God as well as others that I have sinned (Psalm 51).

> You can't bypass repentance to get to grace.

You can't bypass repentance to get to grace. Christ is manifest in our humility, not in our disobedience. Our disobedience cost Jesus everything. Payment for sin always means blood—Christ's blood. And grace does not erase my need for the law.

But what is wrong with me that I keep on committing sin after sin, even as a believer, even as one who knows better? If repentance unto life is my threshold to God, why do I make such plodding progress in growing to be like Jesus?

Why Do Christians Still Sin?

Sometimes I wish that all birthday and holiday wrapping paper would have this printed on it: *Lower Your Expectations, Increase Your Joy*. Seriously. I coined this phrase long before God gave me children, and children started coveting everything each Pixar movie promised. In fact, I started to confront my problem with unreasonable expectations when I was first converted. It seemed to me that there is a difference between standards (the law of God, or the highpoint of knowledge about doctrine as portrayed in the Bible) and expectations (our ability to live up to this on our own terms).

I realized that my problem with shame was a problem with (my) expectations, not with (God's) standards. I expected that

Christians ought not to struggle with sin if we were truly converted. I expected that all of my sinful feelings ought to go away now that I am in Christ. I expected that knowing better should solve the problem of the repeat offense of sin. But after I was converted, it seemed like my struggle with sin was just ramping up. And, my pastor and church friends were discipling me to understand that the book of Romans, especially chapters 5–7, explained why. So, why do Christians still struggle with sin if we are new creatures for whom the old has passed away (2 Cor. 5:17)?

Truly, one of the most maddening and confusing realities Christians face is why we continue to sin. Do we choose it? Does sin still abide in believers? If we are new creatures in Christ, why aren't we simultaneously converted and sanctified in a complete and satisfying way? If God loves us, why doesn't he change our sinful desires comprehensively? Why do believers still sin? And how could my deepest desires be sinful, when they are inseparable from my sense of self, when they themselves form a reality of selfhood that diffuses into character, not claiming a discrete turf in my heart, but claiming all that I experience?

Put another way: If grace is supposed to heal me, why am I still stuck and sick? Has God passed me over? Does God not hear my prayers?

There are two different Christian views on this conundrum of why believers sin. The dominant evangelical position says that God's solution to shame is the full knowledge that we are new creatures in Christ. Beg for more grace. But don't even try to obey the law because you are doomed to failure. And failure, declares this theology, is virtuous, inevitable, and good, as it shows forth God's grace. Failure has become, as Jen Wilkin says, a virtue.[2] Her excellent blog piece exposes the danger of this new glamorization of failure.

There is not one moment in the Bible where we see failure as a virtue. And anyone who conflates humility with failure fails to understand the importance of the first term and the seriousness of the second. A Reformed position offers a different perspective on the problem of why believers sin, and with this perspective, a different solution. Represented by the Puritan John Owen, a

Reformed evangelical position teaches us that sin dwells within us (called indwelling sin) and continues in the life of a new creature. Sin must be dealt with in a posture of Christian combat, not in expected or celebrated defeat and failure. We are to use the full armor of all of the means of grace that God gives to us. This position teaches us that conversion gives you freedom from the crime of sin and gives you liberty to respond to God's grace of conversion through repentance and obedience. Conversion gives you the freedom to repent, not the freedom to expect failure. It was then that I got it: repentance and the love for God—and the obedience to his law that grows from them—were the missing links between shame and grace.

It may seem like I am being *schismatic* here, pitting one theological posture over and against the other. After all, can't we just agree that we all love Jesus?

Yes, I believe that all people who call themselves Christian love Jesus. Both Christians who cry for more grace and Christians who cry for deeper repentance love Jesus. But sadly, we don't necessarily agree on who he is and what he has done. And this is a very big problem. There is simply no getting around it: our theology matters a lot.

Schismatic— causing division.

Let's turn to 2 Corinthians 5:17: "Therefore, if anyone is in Christ, he is a new creature; the old things passed away; behold, new things have come." A Reformed theology reminds us that new creatures in Christ must mortify the flesh and put to death those sinful desires of the flesh and of the world that entice us (Rom. 8:13). In so doing, we see that grace equips us for the kind of war that renounces sin. Repentance is both an art and an ongoing spiritual practice, and it will continue until Jesus returns or we die and are glorified. The old man inside us, while dead, is like a tree cut at the root: it still sprouts a few green leaves. Or, in the words of the old magician in the movie *The Princess Bride*, the sin that abides in us after conversion is only "mostly dead."

Expectations matter. And so do standards.

Because of our fallen natures, we expect that we will be repenting of sin until glory. But repentance is not simply proof of failure. It is, more importantly, a sign of God's hand upon us. It is a conversion proof, as only a saved person can repent of sin. Because of God's righteousness, we honor his standards for holiness by vigilantly putting to death all idols and by refusing to be idol-makers, even when it means getting a different job (and one with less prestige), choosing better friends, or throwing away your smartphone.

Why Can't We All Just Get Along? Why Make Such a Big Deal about Sin?

John Owen says that sin abides in and acts in the lives of new creatures in Christ, and the first and most salient work of all believers is the mortification, or killing, of it. Paul's poignant cry in Romans 7:15–17 foregrounds this doctrine: "For what I am doing, I do not understand; for I am not practicing what I would like to do, but I am doing the very thing that I hate. But if I do the very thing thing I do not want to do, I agree with the Law, confessing that the Law is good. So now, no longer am I the one doing it, but sin which dwells in me." Let's ponder this.

Even though I am a new creature in Christ, I still struggle with my old nature.

I see God's grace in his convicting me of my sin and becoming sin on my behalf so that I can be crucified with him and rise again:

Therefore we have been buried with Him through baptism into death, so that as Christ was raised from the dead through the glory of the Father, so we too might walk in newness of life. (Rom. 6:4)

I attest that the law is good because it causes me to flee to Christ for salvation. Thus, I am saved by grace alone, and not by works:

For by grace you have been saved through faith; and that not of yourselves, it is the gift of God.... (Eph. 2:8)

Sin thrives in the way that God declared in Genesis 4:7: it has agency, it knows my name, it lurks, it seeks me out, and it dwells in and with me.

And, I am a believer.

Like it or not, because I stand in the covenant of grace, I must mortify my sin. Because I stand in the covenant of grace I am able to mortify sin. Daily. Hourly. No matter how long this sin has been my companion. I must never become sentimental about it. I'm called by God to put it to death. And one big proof that the grace of God is at work in me is that I *know* that I need to do this, even if I can't imagine how.

But is this internal war that I feel between the old Rosaria and the new Rosaria biblical?

John Owen says yes. He tells me to expect to go to war with myself, with my old nature.

But Jeff VanVonderen says no, and calls this idea "Satan's Con." He writes:

> The idea of having two natures at war within the believer is Satan's Con…. The battle is not between two me's. I am not at war with the Spirit of God either. The struggle in the Christian life is that of *choosing* whether to walk by the Spirit or by the flesh.[3]

We are left with two opposing conclusions from Christians about what ails us: Is the war I feel in myself a ploy of the Devil, or is there something vital about my sin nature that I must understand in order to walk in Christian liberty? Is this war I feel inside a lie of the Devil or a truth of Christ? The division is pretty stark here! Am I failing to apprehend the grace God has freely extended by not *choosing* to walk in the Spirit? Does the Bible tell me to expect failure and beg for more grace? And if the problem is that I need more grace, what does repentance of sin really mean? When I sin as a believer, am I trampling upon the blood of my Savior or am I glorifying God in my failure?

This is an important question, because as I discussed in the previous chapter, Satan is a real enemy, and he deceives and he accuses. But is the war that I feel between my old self and my redeemed one a ploy of the Devil or a battle of Christian life for which the Bible through the power of the Holy Spirit prepares and equips me to fight? Do we need more grace or a better handle on the law?

One problem with not knowing how to reconcile the law/ grace landscape is it leaves a person with two competing ways to deal with sin: admitting it, on the one hand, or confessing it, on the other.

The Difference Between Admitting and Confessing Sin
Admitting Sin

Sometimes we think that *admit*[4] merely means telling the truth or stating the obvious or making something known that we would rather not disclose. It helps, though, to realize that the word itself implies that the agent gives access to the reality that he experiences. In other words, to admit implies that you know what you did or felt was not right; maybe even you know that the Bible calls those feelings or deeds sinful, but you also know that the beating heart of this sin lives too deep inside you to disengage. Perhaps you believe that this is just you, just how you are hardwired, and because you believe that there is nothing that you can do about it, you choose to live at peace with yourself. Or perhaps you have been crafting this sin for decades, and its idolatry has made you its slave. Because you know you would lose your reputation if you came clean, you just try to do a better job of hiding it from view.

> Admit—to suffer to enter; to grant entrance, whether into a place, or an office, or into the mind or consideration.

This lived reality is important when it comes to the problem of sin. If I say, "I am just a hot-headed Italian and I can't help myself when I unleash my anger on my children and family," I am not merely expressing that I struggle with, say, losing my temper and saying things in anger. I am also indicating that, in some way, I am entertaining this aspect of my personality as endemic to who I am, not what sin has made of me. I am, on some level, granting the sin of anger an entrance into my identity. But if

I am a believer, is sin "who I am" or is it something else? And if I say, "I am a new creature in Christ and therefore I just need more grace to deal with this, but if God doesn't provide this, it is his fault," the game is lost before the runners line up at the starting line, as this attitude takes me off the hook of ownership of sin.

Our sin both precedes us and then dogs us, and it doesn't really matter if we have a good reason to sin. That's how the Bible explains it. So the first question we must ask ourselves is this: from whose point of view should I approach my sin? The default point of view for all people born after Sigmund Freud is the personal one. Our culture resoundingly believes that life is to be interpreted from the point of view of how I feel and perceive things. This explains in part why we have become a Christian culture that admits sin rather than confesses it, and doesn't linger long enough at the cross to know the difference.

Freud—Sigmund Freud (1856–1939) is the founder of psychoanalysis.

When God approaches Cain after he rejects his sacrifice, God says this: "Why are you angry? And why has your countenance fallen? If you do well, will not your countenance be lifted up? And if you do not do well, sin is crouching at the door; and its desire is for you, but you must master it" (Gen. 4: 6–7). God does not take Cain's point of view into account when he rejects his sacrifice. God does not reconsider his position because of Cain's intentions. A sacrifice must bleed in order to count. This bedrock truth can only be apprehended through God's point of view, not my own good intentions. So instead God rebukes Cain for pouting, and warns him that if he does not change, worse things are in store. God proclaims to Cain something vital about this enemy we call sin: it lurks at the entrance of your life, it knows you and desires you, it has a key to your heart and affections, and you must go to battle with it. Every day.

But if all we do is admit to our sin, we call a deadly truce. The truce is deadly because it is one-sided. We may lay down the weapons of spiritual warfare (Eph. 6:10–17), but Satan doesn't, and our own natural corruption degenerates even deeper. If we value our point of view over God's, we will be deceived and betrayed, as sin never takes a Sabbath rest. When we only admit a problem or concern or difference or something about us that we know is not right, we posture in blame shifting, wanting a watching world to see that this problem we have is of no choice of our own and therefore, at least from our point of view, should not be something whose responsibility we should have to burden.

Part of this is true. We do not choose our sin natures. We do not choose the way that Original Sin leaves a fingerprint on our desires. But when all we do is admit our sin, we reject the biblical concept that Original Sin renders me both corrupt and guilty. When we reject Original Sin, we deny the suffering of Jesus on the cross, who paid our ransom because we could not.

Confessing Sin

Compare this understanding of admitting sin to the definition of *confess.*[5] When we confess sin, we own it. This means that sin does not come with a defense attorney who provides all of the excuses for why what God calls sin is really a grace in my life. It means that just because I like to think of myself as a hot-headed Italian does not mean that God gives me a free pass to yell at my kids. It means that my propensity to yell is not even related to my national heritage, but rather to my heritage in Adam. I yell because I am a sinner, and for no other reason.

Confess—to own, acknowledge, or avow, as a crime, a fault, a charge, or a debt.

Psalm 51 is my guide to what confession looks like. This is a psalm that we often sing before taking the Lord's Supper. David penned it after the Holy Spirit used Nathan to convict David of a bundle of sins: adultery, murder, and deception. When confronted with my sin, a confessing spirit declares as David did in Psalm 51:

> *2–3 Wash me thoroughly from my iniquity and cleanse me from my sin. For I know my transgressions, and my sin is ever*

before me. Here David knows his transgressions. He knows that his sin was treason against a holy God, and that God alone can forgive him.

4 You are justified when You speak and blameless when You judge. David is not making excuses or trying to defend his motives. He knows that God is blameless and right in his assessment of sin.

5 Behold, I was brought forth in iniquity and in sin my mother conceived me. David knows that he was born in Adam, and that his natural inclination is to sin. This is not an excuse. It is reality.

10–13 Create in me a clean heart, O God, and renew a steadfast spirit within me. Do not cast me away from your presence and do not take your Holy Spirit from me. Restore to me the joy of your salvation and sustain me with a willing spirit. Then I will teach transgressors Your ways, and sinners will be converted to You. We see here in these verses a microcosm of the fruit of confession in the Christian life: God creates and recreates; God restores joy in our salvation; God sustains us with his Spirit; God uses our repentance to draw others to him.

The psalm concludes with David recalling an important attribute of God—"A broken and contrite heart, O God, You will not despise" (v. 17). God wants our confession of sin. That gives him glory. We become safe for ministry when we confess and repent. The psalm ends with a prayer that God will build the church: "By Your favor, do good to Zion; build the walls of Jerusalem" (v. 18). Confession of sin moves mountains.

Psalm 32 adds additional insight into God's forgiveness of sin and our repentance. This psalm begins, "Blessed is he whose transgression is forgiven, whose sin is covered!" In repentance, God takes our sin away, and in faith, God clothes us (covers us) in Christ's righteousness. When God covers our sin, we are given deliverance. When we cover our sin through denial or excuse-making, God's hand is heavy upon us. And God's heavy hand is a blessing! It is a sign of his love that he does not leave us in deception: "For day and night Your hand was heavy upon me" (v. 4). When we admit or toy with our sin, God's hand is heavy. When we confess our sin, God's hand moves to bear us up: "I said, 'I will confess my transgression to the Lord,' and you forgave the iniquity of my sin" (v. 5, ESV).

Iniquity is a strong word.

Iniquity is a strong word: it stands for an act of injustice. My sin is an act of injustice against a holy God. But when I confess this, the trustworthy and dependable response from God to my repentance is that God becomes my covering, my hiding place. He preserves my life, establishes my integrity, and gives me peace, purpose, and liberty.

This is even true with sins of personality or appetite. When we confess a sin, we are not asking that God or others see it from our point of view, from the vantage point of our intentions or our motives. Instead, we use God's point of view. We submit to the righteous hand of God. We consent that the Bible is true and that the law of God condemns us. And this either drives us into mad depression or into the open arms of our Savior, Jesus Christ. The implications are far-reaching. Confession of sin is meant to drive us to Christ, for our good and for his glory.

But Christians who indulge the habit of admitting rather than confessing sin over time tend not to see their sin as sin at all. It just seems like life. At first, they may hate the sin. They may truly wish to be free of it. These brothers and sisters may be forgetting or not knowing that even in our battle with sin God gives us an opportunity to glorify him. Indeed, I believe that the job of a Christian is to glorify God in all situations, including in the repentance of sin.

The business of the Christian is not to desire just enough grace to be strong in ourselves. Indeed, strong personalities can and do make behavioral changes on the grounds of will, many of these for the good of their health and well-being. But there is no new life found in the fruit of a self-willed behavioral change. Only the risen Lord can give new life. What separates the admitting of sin from the confession of sin is the cross of Christ. And to unbelievers, the cross is a confusing distraction, a piddling annoyance, not the preeminent triumph of the Creator and Redeemer of life that trumps all empires of the world. We come to the cross in repentance, and it is at the cross that we are, over time and affliction, transformed, partly here on earth, but completely in glory (1 John 3:2; 2 Cor. 3:18).

As believers, what makes us "us" is not that we all struggle with lust or anger or laziness or sex addiction. What makes us "us" is that we have been broken in our sin, and we find our identity in the risen Christ. In John 15:4, Jesus declares, "Abide in Me, and I in you. As the branch cannot bear fruit of itself unless it abides in the vine, so neither can you unless you abide in Me." At the moment that we become a Christian, we are given both the privilege and blessing of union with Christ through the power of the Holy Spirit. This union is permanent, irreversible, and eternal. This union with Christ helps us to see the need for radical repentance. Repentance keeps the branch and the vine indelibly linked.

If our motive in confessing sin is growing in Christ, we will grow in two ways: humility over how impossible it is to battle sin alone, and victory over the compelling seduction of our choice sins. Framing sin from the point of view of our intentions and motives does not palliate the problem or improve our standing with God or man. Why? Because sin is not my personal problem or shortcoming. Sin is, in the words of *The Westminster Shorter Catechism*, "any want of conformity unto, or transgression of, the law of God" (Q. 14).[6] Sin is mutiny, either by its omission ("want of conformity to") or its commission ("transgression of the law of God").

It is the moral anesthetic of our day to ask God and our friends to only understand our sin from our point of view. This mind-set of seeing sin from a personal point of view has led to, at best, weak Christians crippled by sin and untouched by gospel power, or at worst, wolves in sheep's clothing who hunker down with offices in the church, teaching feeble sheep a perverted catechism, one that renders sin grace and grace sin, one that confuses doubt with intelligence and skepticism with renewed hope. When we live by the belief that sin is best discerned from our own point of view, we cannot help but to develop a theology of excuse-righteousness. We become anesthetized to the reality of our own sin. One consequence of this moral anesthesia is the belief that you are in good standing with God if you give to him what the desires of your flesh can spare. But sin, biblically rendered, is both a crime and a disease, requiring both the law of God and his grace to apply it for true help.

Puritan Theology: A Blast of Fresh Air for Diagnosing Sin

As I was searching for someone to explain to me what repentance really involved, I came across a book by Thomas Watson entitled *The Doctrine of Repentance*,[7] first published in 1668 and reprinted in a series called *Puritan Paperbacks*. In its pages I found a true friend, someone who also found joy and union in Christ through radical and constant repentance. This is how I first made friends with Puritan theology.

Puritan theology refers to a sixteenth- and seventeenth-century movement that spanned two continents and focused on three distinct values:

1) union with our triune God in mind, emotion, and identity;

2) Reformed and confessional theology, endorsing a systematic understanding of the Scriptures that pervades personhood and politics;[8]

3) a love for reforming the church in worship, faith, and practice.

What I love about the Puritans is that their doctrines of sin and grace provide a perfect balance. Puritans are realistic about the human condition. They viewed sin as more evil than hell itself, and they examined sin in its three forms: *original, actual,* and *indwelling*.

Doesn't that sound extreme to our ears? How can sin (which we commit daily) be worse than hell (where those who reject and hate God experience eternal torment)? The first thing you notice when you ask a question like this is that the observation implies that it is God's point of view, not our own, that matters.

Why is sin worse than hell?[9] In hell, the consciousness of the soul is manifest and alert to the truth. As in the biblical parable of the rich man and Lazarus (Luke 16:19–25), the rich man is tormented in hell for the crime of his unbelief and unfaithfulness. He had a hard heart towards God and felt no remorse for the suffering of Lazarus. Now in hell, he knows it: "In Hades, he lifted up his eyes, being in torment, and saw Abraham far away and Lazarus on his bosom. And he cried out and said, 'Father Abraham, have mercy on me, and send Lazarus so that he may dip the tip of his finger in water and cool off my tongue, for I am in agony in this flame'" (vv. 23–24). When Abraham rejects this request, explaining the law that heaven and hell divide by an uncrossable chasm, the rich man begs for the souls of his brothers. Even souls in hell indirectly make known God's glory by revealing their conscious understanding of their evil. Hell is evidence that every knee will bow.

So, why is sin worse than hell? Hell vindicates God as our righteous judge, while sin separates us from him.

Sin: Original, Actual, and Indwelling

Anthony Burgess (not the same guy who authored *A Clockwork Orange*) wrote a powerful volume on sin, entitled *The Doctrine of Original Sin Asserted and Vindicated against the Old and New Adversaries Thereof*. In this book, he organizes sin into three categories: original, actual, and indwelling.

For Burgess and the Puritans, Romans 5–7 constituted a "divine map" of the microstudy of sin in the believer's life. Romans 5 outlines Original Sin, and we see in this chapter that it is insidious, imputed, and inherent. Original Sin is one of the most maligned worldviews of our day. Indeed, many evangelicals meet it with uproarious rejection.

Original Sin takes its name from Augustine, who said, "Even infants are born sinners, not by their own act, but because of their origin."[10] About this Alan Jacobs comments, "And here we see what is meant by Original Sin, *peccatum originalis* in Augustine's Latin: sin that is already inside us, already dwelling in us at our origin, at our very conception."[11] Our "origin" is in Adam. And this feels deeply unfair. Our most basic understanding of justice screams out against this. Jacobs says: "We struggle to hold together a model of human sinfulness that is universal rather than local, in which we inherit sin rather than choose it, and in which, nevertheless, we are fully, terrifyingly responsible for our condition."[12]

Wise men rally against this idea. Jean-Jacques Rousseau, philosophical leader of the French Revolution, foregrounded a worldview based on its complete opposite: the free will of man and the belief that the "natural" innocence of children will flourish in a world filled with human creativity and goodness. The nameless creature or monster in Mary Shelley's *Frankenstein* (1818 edition) is a child of the philosophy of Rousseau. He reads all the right books (including Goethe's suicide novel, *The Sorrows of Young Werther*).[13] After he kills in cold blood every human being that his creator loved, this creature born in a laboratory from the mind of a brilliant bachelor, and weaved together with a free will but no God-reflecting soul, laments like this: "I, the miserable and the abandoned, am an abortion, to be spurned at, and kicked, and trampled on. Even now my blood boils at the recollection of this injustice."[14]

If Rousseau is right, then Frankenstein's creature is a hero, for even as he leaves a trail of blood behind him, he has accomplished the self-actualizing task of knowing himself. But indeed, as Randell Jarrell quipped, "Rousseau was wrong: that man, when you knock his chains off, sets up the death camps."[15] It seems that Original Sin is friend or foe depending on how wide your angle is: from the housetops, we see Original Sin as dangerous time and time again. From our navel-gazing, Rousseau seems dead on. Our intentions are noble, we protest. All we need now is more grace! But good intentions do not erase or minimize the way Original Sin distorts us all.

But the story does not stop with Original Sin.

Actual sin, the second type that Burgess unveils, stems from Original Sin and is any transgression of the law of God in "thought, word or deed."[16] Actual sins are transient in comparison to indwelling sins, which Burgess describes as "fixed sins in us, and these habits of sin...strengthen our original corruption."[17] The Puritans believed that sin corrupted, crippled, and contaminated both believers and unbelievers, but not in the same way. A believer cannot die from the crime of sin (as an unbeliever can), but if he is not in constant and effective battle with sin, a believer will die of its disease, of the way that it ravages his conscience and relationships and even perhaps body.

> Noetic—from the Greek *nous*, referring to the mind, mindfulness, and the ability to think and reason.

Sin in the unregenerate is often referred to as having a *noetic* effect. In the unregenerate, sin corrupts knowledge as it does not lead the knower to his Maker. John Owen says it best: "The knowledge of a proud man is the throne of Satan in his mind."[18]

Indwelling sin, the third type, always abides in us for as long as we live in this world, and for that reason we must constantly be mortifying it. Because it always abides, we must never speak as though we had "already obtained it or…already become perfect" (Phil. 3:12). Not only does indwelling sin abide, it also lives and acts and "labors to bring forth the deeds of the flesh."[19] It seeks to destroy us, not merely allow us to dabble with unpleasantries. Indwelling sin has agency and evil intent, and it knows where we live. Mortifying indwelling sin is the Christian's daily battle. Later in this chapter I will talk about how to respond to this pernicious but intimate adversary.

What causes us to sin? Temptation. What is temptation? From where does it originate, and how ought the believer to gain victory over it?

Is temptation my friend or my foe?

Temptation

Oswald Chambers says that "temptation fits the nature of the one tempted, and reveals the possibilities of the nature…. Temptation yielded to is lust deified" (*My Utmost for His Highest*, September 17 entry). Temptation comes in many forms, but it is always personal, uncannily tailor-made for our individual moral weakness, and it takes aim at God's character, seeking to ransack our faith.

In Matthew 26:41, our Lord commands this: "Keep watching and praying that you may not enter into temptation." From this verse we know that temptation is an alluring evil or a moral test.

Although temptation is not sin itself, it is also not good.

Although temptation is not sin itself, it is also not good. Temptation is a mighty antagonist. In addition, we know from Scripture that the means of prevention is watching and praying.

Truth be told, watching and praying seem like a pathetic counterattack. But that is because we underestimate the spiritual armor that God gives his sons and daughters.

Since the Bible offers two distinct words that shape our understanding of human nature—temptation and sin—any worldview that attempts to understand human nature without taking these into account will fundamentally distort and deny what it means to be human.

John Owen brings helpful detail to our discussion about sin and temptation. According to Owen, temptation is "any thing, state, way, or condition that, upon any account whatsoever, has a force or efficacy to seduce, to draw the mind and heart of a man from its obedience, which God requires of him, into any sin, in any degree of it whatsoever."[20] Note that any temptation can lead a person into *any* sin. It is a force. And forces must be reckoned with, not passively accepted.

God does not tempt (James 1:12–15) and Jesus was tempted in all ways, but did not sin (Heb. 4:15). James 1:14–15 says this:

Teleological—concerning the ultimate end or purpose of a thing.

"Each one is tempted when he is carried away and enticed by his own lust. Then when lust has conceived, it gives birth to sin, and when sin is accomplished, it brings forth death." Temptation is not something to be celebrated. It originates with Satan and its desired end is to cause sin and separation from God. Desire can have a range of syntactical meanings in the Bible, but in these passages, it refers to something internal that entices a believer to want something he ought not have. Desire for evil things that is *teleological* is predatory and sinful—it will not be quenched until its object has been consumed. This is the kind of desire James refers to in these verses, the kind of desire that the King James Version and New American Standard Bible translate in James 1:14–15 as *lust*. Temptation, then, puts each and every one of us in a dangerous dilemma, and we do not know when it first entices us if we will be victors or victims.

In the book of Hebrews, we are told that Jesus was tempted. What does temptation mean to Jesus? Did his sinlessness mean that temptation for Jesus was not as bad as it is for us? In Hebrews 2:18 we read, "For since He Himself was tempted in that which He has suffered, He is able to come to the aid of those who are tempted." This is a key verse. Linking temptation with suffering, we see that from the point of view of Scripture, temptation is never to be exonerated, celebrated, or minimized. It is never to become an accolade or a defining marker of who we are.

In Hebrews 4:15 we read, "For we do not have a high priest who cannot sympathize with our weaknesses, but One who has been tempted in all things as we are, yet without sin." And Hebrews 5:8 reads, "Although He was a Son, He learned obedience from the things which He suffered." While Jesus was tempted, Jesus was not born with a sin nature. That means that the evil that enticed him came from someplace other than his own nature. Put in the positive, it means that because he was fully holy, he would meet temptation all the way to its finished end of victory. It means that in his feelings and experiences, Jesus, while tempted, never crossed the line into sin, and conquered that temptation with perfect obedience.

This raises the question of how Jesus could be both man and God. It begs the question if the Son and the Father shared one divine will. The early church resolved this question in 451 AD with the Nicene Creed and then gave further clarification in 680 AD with the Third Council of Constantinople. The early church confirmed that Jesus had one nature, but two wills: one divine and the other human. As Mark Jones points out in a most helpful book, *A Christian's Pocket Guide to Jesus Christ: An Introduction to Christology*,[21] "Christ would not be properly human if his will was divine…. Christ's human will was necessary for him to render true obedience in the place of his people."[22] Christ's human will meant that his body, while sinless, felt the infirmities and corruptions of the world. He needed food and rest and friendship. At the same time, as Jones writes, "Christ's…obedience to the will of his Father was obedience arising out of love for God with his human heart, soul, mind and strength." We see this tension in John 6:38 ("For I have come down from heaven, not to do My own will, but the will of Him who sent me") and John 10:17 ("For this reason the Father loves Me, because I lay down my life so that I may take it up again"). Donald Macleod describes Christ's battle with temptation like this: "He felt the appeal of the sinful proposals put to Him and He had to struggle with all his might to repel them."[23] But because Christ was not born in Adam, he had no internal sin nature and therefore no fallen desires that originated from within.

For some, this inherent sinlessness makes Christ's temptations seem insincere, as his holiness seems to set up the game in a way that would make any empathy he might have for my temptation shallow. If we think like this, we are missing an important point.

Christ was truly tempted. On earth, Christ was not *omniscient*, according to his human nature. He relied on the Holy Spirit for power. He had to trust in God, exercise faith, and sweat blood.

Omniscient — all knowing.

He was tempted to preserve his life in the wilderness (Luke 4) and in the garden (Matt. 26), but he met that temptation with faith in God and obedience, choosing the Father's will over his own. He modeled for us what we should desire in the face of temptation: to choose the Father's will over our own. Because he had a human will while he physically walked on earth, Jesus can truly empathize with our temptation. His empathy rests not in desiring sinful things (which is more often than not our problem with temptation), but in choosing the Father's will over his own. His agonizing garden prayer embodies this. Matthew 26 tells us this:

> 39 And He went a little beyond them, and fell on His face, and prayed, saying, "My Father, if it is possible, let this cup pass from Me; yet not as I will, but as You will.

40 And He came to the the disciples and found them sleeping, and said to Peter, "So you men could not keep watch with Me for one hour?
41 Keep watching and praying that you may not enter into temptation; the spirit is willing, but the flesh is weak."
42 He went away again a second time and prayed, saying, "My Father, if this cannot pass away unless I drink it, Your will be done."

With great agony and grief and turmoil that we cannot imagine, Jesus does what we are called to do in face of temptation: to choose God's will over our own. Jesus met temptation with obedience, and that meant going against the natural desires of his human will. He had to do this because if he had not gone to the cross without temptation, he could not have ransomed us from our own sin. He was obeying for the Father's honor and out of sacrificial love for you and me and all of his people.

We depend more on his obedience than we do on his being in the same boat with us. We find our only hope in his sinlessness, knowing that it resulted from a battle with sin that he experienced more deeply than we do. His perfect holiness and obedience in the face of temptation gives us proof of his sacrificial love. He understands the contours of sin and temptation better through his triumph over it than we do in our defeat.

Some people believe that if Jesus did not experience sinful internal desires such as sexual lust, then he isn't fully human. This reveals the tendency to want to make Jesus in our own image. Jesus had intimate surroundings with his disciples. His friendships were deep and intense. He met with the woman at the well alone. But he did not have one unholy sexual thought for any man or woman. His orientation was to obey the Father.

As I am writing this, my children are waging war with lightsabers, and about one hundred stuffed animals being used as ammunition are currently careening through the hallway and encroaching into my office. The children are at the tail end of the head cold that they just gave to me. They are feeling better and I am feeling like an elephant is tap-dancing on my sinuses. Soon the battle, as all battles do, spills over into the out-of-bounds territory of my desk and writing space. Before I know what hit me, a beloved child of the covenant smacks me upside the head with a flashing lightsaber. And now I am just losing it. Really. You would be really ashamed to be me right now. I am screaming for them to stop. Just STOP. I have completely lost all self-control. And they are SO loud, and I am so weak in voice, and the lightsabers make these swooshing sounds when they make contact with something (like my head), that my children can't even hear my protest!

Then I realize it, like another smack upside the head: my anger is sinful anger and God is protecting my children from it. *From me.*

I love them. I love them more than I love writing this book. I want them. I fought for them. I prayed for them before I met them. I pray for them daily and sometimes hourly. I cherish them. But sometimes, dare I say it, as a homeschool mom I fantasize about all of the liberty that yellow school bus that passes my street corner twice a day might offer.

So, what do I do? I go to God immediately with repentance. And then I push *save* on this chapter and get up and correct my children in kindness. They protest. They complain. They feel persecuted. I take away all stuffed animal ammo and all weapons, and I put the children in their separate rooms to read. The whole drama has taken all of ten minutes.

Done.

Quiet.

I return to my desk, and, just for good measure, insert my ear plugs.

You see, immediately as a believer, I must go to the Lord in repentance when feelings cross from temptation to sin. For me, they cross the line a lot. My track record is pathetic. I don't know about you, but I often seem to know the line between temptation and sin when I cross it. While repentance is my threshold to God, obedience was Jesus' threshold to God. Christ's suffering and obedience then become our powerful inspiration.

Psalm 22 harrowingly records the temptation of Jesus on the cross:

> *My God, my God, to you I cry,*
> *O why have You forsaken me?*
> *Why are You far from giving help,*
> *And from my agonizing plea?*
> *All day, my God, I cry in vain;*
> *By night, yet no relief I gain.*[24]

This is a commanding psalm to sing in its entirety before taking the Lord's Supper. As I type these words, I cannot help but pause to sing them. I'm not in good voice from this head cold, but somehow this psalm sounds even more accurately rendered in my weakness.

Indeed, as your voice laments through each stanza, you reflect upon the agony of Christ's will, the cost of his obedience, the effect of his representational love. In the last words of the psalm, you experience the positive application of Christ's sinlessness in face of temptation. Without it, we would not be at the Supper at all:

> *A seed will rise to do His will,*
> *And of the Lord be made aware.*
> *The generation that will come*
> *Will then His righteousness declare,*
> *To people who are yet to be,*
> *That He has done this; it was He.*[25]

Temptation travels on a slippery slope, and the law of gravity in our sin nature renders temptation an easy slide downward, especially if we minimize sin's power to deceive and destroy us on the grounds that we have kept company with it for so long. Not so for Jesus. His nature was pure, and therefore his experience of temptation was different than mine. His experience was fierce and raw. Temptation insulted his divine nature, and bore holes in his human will long before the nails were driven down into his hands. Jesus was tempted in all ways. He therefore can empathize with my feelings.

He reminds me to "Get up and pray that you may not enter into temptation" (Luke 22:46). He commands me to "Watch and pray, that you enter not into temptation" (Matt. 26:41). I am not to watch my own personality or my own indwelling sin or my own good reason for making an idol out of temptations. I am to watch out for the holiness of God, made manifest in me by the shedding of blood. He sweated blood. He withstood the test. He ran the whole race.

We cannot make such claims. We have not been tested that hard, or humiliated that comprehensively. We are in the ABCs of the kindergarten of the school of temptation. By not falling into temptation, Jesus ran the whole race, while I collapsed in the first mile.

It fascinates me that Jesus used an ordinary means of grace to flee Satan's temptations in the wilderness: he used the Word of God. This occurred during his post-baptism, post-fast, desert experience recorded in Matthew 4:1–11. Satan tempted Jesus to turn stones into bread, hurl himself from the pinnacle of the temple, and worship the Antichrist. Each time, Jesus protected himself with the shield of the Word. Why? Why did Jesus use something ordinary—something that we believers possess—instead of some extraordinary God-infused gift? To show in his mercy the true sufficiency of Scripture. To reveal that Jesus met temptation in the wilderness as a man and in the power of the Holy Spirit.

He also did this to show something important about the nature of temptation: it's not primarily about us. That's right. If you are in Christ, temptation is not about some essential truth or inherent wisdom about us—and therefore should not become a term of selfhood, self-representation, or identity. It is about warfare. And for Christians, it is about our allegiance to Christ in this war. Russell Moore says this:

> Temptation is so strong in our lives precisely because it's not
> about us. Temptation is an assault by the demonic powers

on the rival empire of the Messiah. That is why conversion to Christ doesn't diminish the power of temptation—as we often assume—but only ratchets it up.[26]

Making an identity out of temptation is like putting on the opposing team's jersey at a ball game and then taking to the field: it is confusing, deceptive, and dangerous. How do we make an identity out of temptation? By collapsing what you desire with who you are. By collapsing what tempts you or what trips you up with who you will become.

If you don't believe this, then just think about what representation means: it means to re-present, to present again for all of posterity. We who are washed by the blood of Christ are "buried with Him through baptism into death" (Rom. 6:4). Thus, believers wear the same team colors. We may struggle with different patterns of desire, but because temptation is not about us, temptation does not define us. We are covered and washed by the blood of Christ alone. To say, "temptation is not a sin, therefore my temptation pattern is morally neutral or even sanctifiable" is misguided and dangerous. It shows that we have embraced an identity that contradicts God's revealed purpose. God's revealed purpose for my identity always nails me to his cross.

A Believer's Main Business: The Mortification of Sin

If temptation is not a sin, what is sin? G. K. Chesterton makes sin analogous to a rhinoceros, and says this: "If a rhinoceros was to enter this restaurant now, there is no denying he would have great power here. But I should be the first to rise and assure him that he had no authority whatever."[27] Like a rhino, sin has power without authority, but it can bully and sucker-punch the strongest Christian into doing its bidding. The Bible graciously records how heroes of the faith have fallen through the floor of temptation into sin, in part to show us that God's grace is ever available to a believing and repenting heart. Again: temptation is not a sin. But what you do with it may be.

The Bible tells us that when a sinful desire has taken root in our heart, and when it takes on a life and agency of its own, even if we are not acting upon it, we are dealing with an indwelling sin. Pornography addicts who begin by writing erotica and go on to commit adultery did not speak their marriage vows while thinking they would ever be unfaithful. They thought, like we all do when we are in the throes of deception, that we have our sin under control. Sin starts oh-so gently. We dangle our toes over the inviting water decades before we plunge ourselves—and our loved ones—into the open-mouthed depths of the raging sea in a murderous storm.

The Bible's solution to sin is confession and repentance—accomplished only through God's redemptive grace—and, through the blood of Christ, the mortification of sin, including the sin of my most cherished and primal feelings.

But God does not leave us in the grave, with only the mortification of our sin for company. Psalm 40:2 declares, "He brought me up out of the pit of destruction, out of the miry clay, and He set my feet upon a rock, making my footsteps firm." God gives us the grace to repent and mortify our sins, to be sure. Christ gives us empathy; he knows what we endure.

Vivifies—enlivens or makes alive.

By his death, he gave himself to us as a ransom for our sins. And by his resurrection, he gives us the hope and promise of a new life, "born again to a living hope through the resurrection of Jesus Christ from the dead" (1 Peter 1:3). In Owen's (and before him, John Calvin's) terms, we *mortify* our sins through his grace working in us, and he *vivifies* our new life. Mortification refers to putting off the "old man," and vivification embodies the idea of being born again, given a new heart by the power of the Holy Spirit. Yes, we were all born in sin. That is why we must be born again. In Owen's words, "The Holy Spirit works in us and upon us as we are fit to be wrought in and upon; that is, so as to preserve our own liberty and free obedience. He works upon our understandings, wills, consciences, and affections, agreeably to our own natures; he works in us, and with us, not against us or without us."[28] The majestic balm of life in Christ "by grace alone" embraces sanctification as both putting off sin and renewal in grace. And we walk in liberty.

One very difficult aspect about sin is that my sin never feels like sin to me. My sin feels like life, plain and simple. My heart is an idol factory and my mind an excuse-making factory, especially when it comes to dealing with the kind of sin that clobbers me the most—indwelling sin—the unrelenting, ever-present kind that never takes a Sabbath and that Paul references in Romans 7: "So now, no longer am I the one doing it, but sin which dwells in me" (v. 17); "But if I am doing the very thing I do not want, I am no longer the one doing it, but sin which dwells in me" (v. 20).

John Owen confronts this in his work *The Nature, Power, Deceit, and Prevalency of the Remainders of Indwelling Sin in Believers*, first published in 1635. I believe that this is the most important book for contemporary Christians to read.[29] Owen's work is divided into three parts:

Part 1: The Nature of Indwelling Sin;
Part 2: The Power and Efficacy of Indwelling Sin;
Part 3: The Effect and Strength of Indwelling Sin.

This is a book to read slowly and prayerfully. It disarms as it explains the unexplainable: How can I be a new creature in Christ and have sin dwell in my heart? How can my mind be redeemed, and yet still I struggle with this fallen nature? How can I pray and fast over decades and still wake up to the same old me with the same old sin? As Kris Lundgaard, author of *The Enemy Within*, puts it: "Sin can be like trick birthday candles: you blow them out and smile, thinking you have your wish; then your jaw drops as they burst into flames."[30]

So, how do you fight an enemy that has climbed over the wall and is now in the house? Owen recommends doing these four things:

1) *Starve it.* That's right. Indwelling sin is a parasite, and it eats what you do. The Word is poison to sin when embraced by a heart made new by the Holy Spirit. You starve indwelling sin by feeding yourself deeply on the Word of God. Sin cannot abide in the Word. So, fill your hearts and minds with Scripture. Psalm singing, for me, is powerful devotional practice as it melts

Scripture memory into my soul with each note. Psalm singing helps me to use everything I have to fold my will into God's Word. Psalm selections take up large parts of a whole chapter of Scripture, and singing psalms is one way to take in the Bible in large portions and to memorize a whole book of the Bible over time. We benefit from reading the Bible comprehensively, big chunks and whole books at a time. This allows us to see God's providence at work in big-picture ways.

Don't make excuses. Don't get sentimental about sin.

2) *Call sin what it is.* Don't "admit" sin as a kind of benign visitor; confess it as an evil offense and put it out! You can't domesticate sin by admitting it into your home. Don't make a false peace. Don't make excuses. Don't get sentimental about sin. Don't play the victim. Don't live by excuse-righteousness. If you bring a baby tiger into your house, buy it a collar and leash, and name it "Fluffy," don't be surprised if you wake up one day and Fluffy is eating you alive. That is how sin works, and Fluffy knows her job. Sometimes sin lurks and festers for decades, deceiving the sinner that he really has it all under control, until it unleashes itself on everything you built, cherished, and loved. Be wise about your choice sins and don't coddle them.

3) *Extinguish indwelling sin.* How? Mortify (kill) it. Sin is not only an enemy, says Owen. Sin is at enmity with God. Enemies can be reconciled, but there is no hope for reconciliation for anything at enmity with God. Anything at enmity with God must be mortified. Our battles with sin draw us closer to union with Christ, and in that way much good comes from dealing with sin God's way. Indeed, as Romans 6 states, our identity comes from being crucified and resurrected with Christ:

> 4 Therefore, we have been buried with him through baptism into death, so that as Christ was raised from the dead through the glory of the Father, so we too might walk in newness of life.
> 5 For if we have become united with Him in the likeness of

His death, certainly we shall also be in the likeness of His resurrection,
6 knowing this, that our old self was crucified with Him, in order that our body of sin might be done away with, so that we would no longer be slaves to sin...

4) *Vivify righteousness and walk in the Spirit.* Cultivate daily your new life in Christ. God does not leave us alone to fight the battle in shame. Instead, through the power of the Holy Spirit, the soul of each believer is "vivified." "To vivicate" means to animate, or to give life to. Vivification (redemption) complements mortification, and by so doing, it allows us to see the wide angle of sanctification. The promise of redemption allows us to visualize ourselves as redeemed men and women. By so doing, it gives shape and form to our identity in Christ, even on this side of eternity.

Sexual sin is often the one that brings whole households and churches into ruin. After a while, people battling sexual sin grow weary. It may seem that God is calling unmarried Christians to be sexually repressed people.

But God's vision of sexuality, what Bible professor and author Christopher Yuan calls *holy sexuality*, is not a white-knuckling, hand-slapping, self-deprecating life practice. Not at all. God is calling us to so greatly love others that we do not desire for them anything that might separate them from God. Holy sexuality is a love so big that it treasures the purity of another, exonerating that person's status as an image bearer or a daughter or son of the King, and not dehumanizing him or her through manipulating lust.

Redemption brings a person beyond obedience to a deeper union with Christ and a greater love for fellow image bearers through self-denial. Killing or mortifying sin is not enough. We must go through this battle to find joy in melting our will with God's, even as God's will often crosses our own. Vivification is an invitation to read all of Scripture not merely as something which gives us good advice, but rather a living text that meets us in our redeemed soul and thereby shapes our desires.

In my experience, this reshaping of desires through the godly gift of redemption is complex and *dialogic*, not flat, singular, and finished. It engages me in a daily back-and-forth that the psalmist does in Psalm 62. This psalm begins with David describing his practice. He says: "My soul waits in silence for God only" (v. 1). By the fifth line, David is not listening to himself and his woes. Instead, he is talking to himself using God's Word. He says, "My soul, *wait* in silence for God only" (v. 5, emphasis mine). David is applying redemptive courage. He is taking himself by the scruff of the neck and telling himself what to do. He knows the sad state of his condition, but he is not causing himself to become more and more depressed by the fact of this. How? He is seeing the facts of his life through the lens of faith that God has given him.

Dialogic — relating to dialogue or conversation.

After he talks to himself (instead of listening to himself), he then talks to himself about who God is. Redemption is the imposition of God's character, will, power, and life into our own, bringing us from death to life. David is not condemning his feelings. He is using his faith to interpret his personal experience. He declares, "Trust in Him at all times, O people; pour out your heart before Him" (v. 8). He is declaring that a saved man is never alone with his problems, and ought not act as though he is. A saved man or woman always has God's kind company.

He concludes the psalm in confidence that even if God will not give him his heart's desires, he can trust that God will answer his prayers rightly: "Once God has spoken; twice I have heard this: that power belongs to God; and lovingkindness is yours, O Lord, for you recompense a man according to his work" (vv. 11–12).

The work to which the psalmist refers is not works-righteousness. It is not white-knuckling it through clobbering temptation with a stubborn will. The work here refers to the counterintuitive power of melting your will with your Maker's through the vivification of the Lord's work.

The work of a believer is responsive, not initiative. We

respond to God's love because we must. Like Peter, when called to do the impossible, we do not look to our limitations, but we ponder this: "Lord, to whom shall we go? You have words of eternal life" (John 6:68). Owen says this: "Mortification of any sin must be by a supply of grace. Of ourselves, we cannot do it."[31] The gospel does not take us halfway there. God takes us all the way home. But if what you seek is grace apart from Christ's blood, you will never get home.

A Biblical Solution to the Problem of Shame

A biblical solution to the problem of shame is a godly understanding of both law and grace, remembering that confession of sin glorifies God,[32] and that the promises in God's covenant with you are a banquet of encouragement. We can model that for one another as we do life together. When Kent proposed to me, I understood that he really could forgive me for the sexual sin of my past. I felt years of sin melt away when Kent showed me by his actions that he did not have higher standards for me than God has. He showed me that he truly believed that repentance brings glory to God. But this is counterintuitive. Only a Christian walking with the kind company of the Holy Spirit could find peace and joy and God's love in repentance of sin.

John Owen also speaks of shame. He says that shame roots not in God failing to understand our weakness, but in ourselves failing to understand God's greatness. Owen says: "A universal respect to all God's commandments is the only preservative from shame."[33] In this way, Owen echoes David, who puts it this way: "Then I shall not be ashamed when I look upon all your commandments" (Ps. 119:6). What stands between one believer feeling shame at hearing that Original Sin makes us corrupt and guilty and another finding peace in this theology?

The problem of shame may be one of doctrine or life or both. Shame may result from your sin or from the sin of someone else that landed on you. It may be that good theology is rendered in harsh and unloving hands. Or it may be that some sins are coddled and hidden (for a while) while others rage like a silent wildfire through the lives of believers. But I believe that the missing link for believers to come together in a healthy understanding of sin is Christian love for God's righteousness and for one another, the kind of love that sticks it out in hard times. I will say more about this love in the last chapter, but for now please know that loyal fellowship of believers is not an "add on" to good doctrine. Fellowship of believers is often the vein through which the Savior's blood pumps us whole and well.

After Pentecost, believers were "continually devoting themselves...to fellowship" (Acts 2:42). In a real Christian community, there is no shame in repentance. Real Christian communities view repentant sinners as God sees them: cleansed and robed in Christ's righteousness. And we know that the battle with sin is not finished until we die or Christ returns. For this reason, "from now on we recognize no one according to the flesh" (2 Cor. 5:16). Redeemed people are not known or recognized according to categories of the flesh.

Many people reject the full understanding of sin (original, actual, and indwelling) because it is credited with causing shame and undue emotional duress. Where is the grace in a gospel that calls my deepest desires and most primal senses of self "sin"? An orthodox understanding of sin has been credited with causing Post Traumatic Stress Disorder (PTSD), depression, self-harm, and suicide, among other tragedies. But this is not the way God orchestrates believers to experience repentance. Repentance is how grace flows to the humble heart (James 4:6). Repentance feels like God lifting the weight of conflict off of your shoulders. It feels freeing to finally see what you did not see before, and liberating to release the anger and shame and self-defensiveness that sin always requires.

Repentance of sin is an honor that adorns royalty.

Even when the consequences are dire, it feels glorious to experience that the Lord's burden is much lighter than that of the world, and his yoke befitting to my nature and capacity. Repentance of sin is an honor that adorns royalty. It is the full expression of Christian liberty, and through the Lord's forgiveness, repentance rings one singular note: peace.

To live without shame, both the nature of God and the nature of man must be held in uncompromising love. We must embrace a true biblical understanding of the nature of redeemed people, and a faithful biblical understanding of the God who made us. If both are not held in the strictest love, other worldly identities creep in and subtly seduce us into serving two masters.

Sometimes, these worldly identities enter into the church intending to be a helpful category, meant to smooth the bridge of understanding among God's people. One such worldly category is the concept of sexual orientation, the idea that people are born with a fixed sexual orientation—gay, straight, or bisexual. But this category is unstable and will not stop changing. We are told that sexual orientation is a true and abiding category of humanity. In the next two chapters, I show how this concept has been harmful to all people, but especially, I believe, to believers who struggle with unwanted homosexual desires.

Sexual Orientation

Freud's Nineteenth-Century Mistake

What is Sexual Orientation?

In a recent blog post, Nick Roen wrote about the experience of walking into a room, seeing "Rick," and feeling that warm feeling deep inside. Nick writes:

> As I noticed Rick with pleasure, the attraction produced all sorts of "I want..." desires in me. One of those desires was a sexual desire. No, I wasn't immediately imagining what it would be like to be in bed with him, but the seed was present. However, I also experienced many heightened desires toward Rick that had nothing to do with sex. I desired to go talk to him, shake his hand, get to know him, laugh with him, and serve him a glass of punch. In other words, not only were the seeds of sexual desire present, but the seeds of desires of friendship, hospitality, emotional intimacy, sacrificial service, and love were there as well. All different desires, all colored by the same initial attraction. It is this experience of persistent attractions toward other men leading to multiple heightened desires that constitutes my definition of SSA (same-sex attraction), experiencing a homosexual orientation, or "being gay." The whole experience, not merely the sexual parts.[1]

In this blog post, Nick captures the common use of the concept of sexual orientation: "an enduring pattern of emotional, romantic, and/or sexual attractions to men, women, or both sexes," as defined by the American Psychological Association (APA). In this post, Nick talks about being sexually attracted to Rick, but also being emotionally and affectionally attracted as well. He talks about how these patterns of attraction to men are "persistent" and that they are best categorized by the ideas of "homosexual orientation," or "being gay." Nick goes on in his essay to talk about how some of these attractions are sexually illicit and must be put to death, and others are morally neutral and/or beneficial and should be allowed to flourish, for both personal good and greater social good. I agree. Nick then explains, though, that the whole experience, the sanctified and the sinful, are all part of his sexual orientation. What Nick says is completely accurate according to the APA's definition of sexual orientation.

Nick is a brother in the Lord and I value him and pray for him. In his writing and in our email correspondence, he has helped me see my own blind spots and errors. Even though we disagree on things, I know that he also prays for me. Importantly, I also know Nick's commitment to living in chastity. But Nick promotes a category of personhood that I believe does all of us more harm than good.

Let me explain why.

Nineteenth Century Origins and the Power of the History of Ideas

The concept of sexual orientation was first used by Freud, and its effect, if not intent, was to radically resituate sexuality from its biblical/creational context to something completely new: the foundational drive that determines and defines human identity. Nothing short of personhood was at stake. By defining humanity according to sexual desires and segregating it according to its gendered object, Freud was—intentionally or not—suppressing the biblical category of being made in God's image, male and female, and replacing it with the psychoanalytic category of sexual identity. In both intent and language usage, Freud took aim at the Bible's authority to diagnose gender and sexuality dysfunctions and prescribe solutions for them. I do not believe that this was an innocent move. Throughout his career, Freud maintained that belief in the God of the Bible was a "universal obsessional neurosis."[2] The category of sexual orientation carries with it a cosmology of personhood that undervalues image bearers of a holy God.

Freud did not come out of nowhere. Ideas shape worldview and worldview shapes culture. Freud was a product of German Romanticism. The Romantic period[3] is typified by an uncontested embrace of personal experience, not merely as self-expression or self-representation, but also as *epistemology* and personal identity (who I am, ontologically).[4]

Epistemology — study of how I know what I know.

Johann Wolfgang von Goethe's suicide memoir, *The Sorrows of Young Werther*, narrated this idea for western culture. *Werther* took Germany by storm in 1774, tragically spawning a number of suicides, while manifesting the idea that personal experience is itself a branch of epistemology. That is, Romanticism claimed that you know truth through the lens of your personal experience, and that no overriding or objective opposition can challenge the primal wisdom of someone's subjective frame of intelligibility. In Romanticism, this knowing and being known is identity-rooted and identity-expressive. Romanticism went beyond a solipsistic me-centered understanding of selfhood. *Solipsism* is the belief that only one's own mind and its properties are sure to exist. Romanticism took this one step further to declare personal feelings and experiences the most reliable measure and means of discerning truth.

Both a theological and philosophical issue is at stake here. The theological issue is the development of a category of personhood that rejects Original Sin. In rejecting Original Sin, the Romantics declared their belief in the inherent divinity and goodness of humanity. The philosophical issue is epistemology and the role of personal experience. Prior to the eighteenth century, experience-as-truth — even in secular contexts — would have met with real life and theological challenges. Even today, experience-as-truth is the lowest form of epistemology.

The nineteenth-century category of sexual orientation reflects Romanticism's claim on epistemology, redefining men and women from people who are made in God's image with souls that will last forever to people whose sexual drives and gender identifications define them and liberate them and set them apart. Indeed, while the Christian maintains that image-bearing is what sets apart humans from animals, the nineteenth century ushered in a new measure of man, one for whom sexuality and sexual pleasure became a defining marker. Thus, "sexual orientation" is what we call a *neologism*, and it creates fictional identities that rob people of their true one: male and female image bearers. Sexual orientation is a word that extends the definition of sexuality beyond its biblical confines. Biblically speaking, sexuality is always teleological—that is, sexual desire implies a desired object and sexual practice implies a necessary outcome. Because the APA's definition of sexual orientation includes nonsexual affection, this re-maps personhood in a way that God does not.

Neologism—a new word or expression, or a new meaning of a word.

Put another way, biblically speaking, there is nothing sinful and nothing "gay" about nonsexual same-sex deep and abiding friendship. Desiring to bring someone a glass of punch or sacrificially helping a friend who needs you is an expression of our image-bearing of a holy God, not our persistent patterns of sexual desire or temptation. We must stop and ask: why would the category of sexual orientation include nonsexual affiliation except for the purpose of defining in a new way what it means to be human? This is no small issue. If we privilege secular categories of personhood over and against God's, we are doubting the Bible's ability to understand humanity, and we are denying to ourselves our Maker's instruction. Freud did not invent or discover or name something true about humanity that the writers of the Bible missed. Categories we use to represent image bearers of a holy God matter. Words, like kitchen washrags, carry and distribute history (and bacteria) with each use, and the category-invention of sexual orientation brings much bacteria with it.

Everyone loses when we define ourselves using categories

that God does not. People who identify as heterosexual and homosexual have much to lose. In 2014, Michael Hannon wrote an absorbing essay in the journal *First Things* entitled "Against Heterosexuality: The Idea of Sexual Orientation is Artificial and Inhibits Christian Witness."[5] He begins his essay with Michel Foucault, the famous French historian of ideas who died of AIDS in 1980. Hannon writes:

> Michel Foucault...details the pedigree of sexual orientation in his *History of Sexuality*. Whereas "sodomy" had long identified a class of actions, suddenly for the first time, in the second half of the nineteenth century, the term "homosexual" appeared alongside it. This European neologism was used in a way that would have struck previous generations as a plain category mistake, designating not actions, but people—and so also with its counterpart and foil "heterosexual"...with secular society rendering classical religious beliefs publicly illegitimate, pseudoscience stepped in and replaced religion as the moral foundation for venereal norms.[6]

Sexuality moved from verb (practice) to noun (people), and with this grammatical move, a new concept of humanity was born—the idea that we are *oriented* or framed by our sexual desires; that our differing sexual desires and different objects of desire made up separate species of people, and that self-representation and identity rooted now in sexual orientation, and not in the purposes of God for his image bearers. In Foucault's words, "Homosexuality appeared as one of the forms of sexuality...when it was transposed from the *practice* of sodomy into a kind of interior androgyny, a hermaphrodism of the soul. The sodomite had been a temporary aberration; the homosexual was a new species"[7] (emphasis mine). Prior to the nineteenth century category-invention of sexual orientation, no one's sexual practice or sexual desire prescribed personhood or defined their personal identity.

Notice Foucault's use of the words *form, soul,* and *species.* The use of the word *form* implies that sexual desire shapes our organizing frame, the basic building block of selfhood. The use of the word *soul* implies that sexuality, not God's image, was the real harbinger of humanity. The use of the word *species* means that a new concept of humanity was born, at least within the history of ideas. Sexuality, according to this new definition, exceeds sexual desire. Even in Foucault's articulation, nonsexual affections are catalogued under a person's sexual orientation, thus relocating sexual desire from teleology (its end point) to psychology (personhood, personality, likes, dislikes, etc.). Sexual orientation is thus said to encompass every fiber of a person's selfhood, from margin to center. If I self-define as heterosexual or homosexual, I express that this deep and originating mark of selfhood presents itself in everything I do, from how I walk the dog in the morning, stir the pot of soup at lunch, and take the garbage out at night. With this comprehensive shift in personhood, a new kind of sexual freedom emerged, where everything, including nonsexual affection, is subsumed by this new humanity of sexuality, and everything is a character trait that flows from this humanity of sexuality.

Indeed, sexual orientation went from a categorical invention to heralded immortal truth in one hundred years, taking out the concept of being created in God's image and bearing an eternal soul in its wake. It is now a term embraced uncritically by believers and unbelievers alike. Sexual orientation defines selfhood as the sum-total of our fallen human desires. Through it, we get no glimpse of how the covenant of grace defends our real identity in Christ, or why, say, biblical marriage is a God-designed creation ordinance and a living reflection of Christ and the church, and not merely a man-made convenience.

Heterosexual Blindness and Comparative Sin

I believe that sexual orientation is a lose-lose *paradigm* for everyone, but especially if you struggle with unwanted homosexual desires. Hannon, in contrast, thinks that self-described heterosexuals have the most to lose. He writes: "The most pernicious aspect of the orientation-identity system is that it tends to exempt heterosexuality from moral evaluation. If homosexuality binds us to sin, heterosexuality blinds us to sin."[8]

This heterosexual blindness seems to have two forms: excuse-making for sexual sins of a heterosexual bent (pornography, incest, fornication, and adultery), and an excessive, scintillating focus on what gay men do in bed, known in evangelical circles as the "gag reflex."[9] Indeed,

Paradigm— a model or pattern for something that may be copied.

because of the unwitting deceitfulness of the sexual orientation paradigm, we are much more likely to be numb to *heterosexual* sin and excessively focused on *homosexual* sin than we would have been prior to the nineteenth century.

Heterosexual blindness makes a Christian ignorant to the very sins that may destroy him; *homosexual* approval makes a person unable to enter into a gay neighbor's life in a way that God may use to spare him from God's wrath. Both take Christian witness out of the game. This might raise another question: does Paul's observation in Romans 1:26 that homosexual sex is unnatural warrant the conclusion that heterosexual sexual sin (such as adultery or pornography) is a less heinous form of sin? John Murray's commentary on the book of Romans has been used to defend this paradigm of comparative sin, as he says this on Romans 1:26: "The implication is that, however grievous is fornication or adultery, the desecration involved in homosexuality is on a lower plane of degeneracy; it is unnatural and therefore evinces a perversion more basic."[10]

Does it necessarily follow that homosexual sexual sin is on a higher plane of evil? The question might be posed like this: is Murray endorsing the paradigm of comparative sin (i.e., comparing your sin to someone else's in order to conclude that yours is not as bad)? Many Christians follow a line of reasoning like Murray's and draw the conclusion that same-sex sin is somehow farther from the reach of God's redemption than other expressions of sexual sin. But pride, lust, bitterness, anger, and a multitude of other sins lie behind our sexual sins in a way that prohibits sweeping generalizations as to the evil of one over and against all others. After all, there are heterosexual perversions and abuses that are unspeakably abhorrent. A heterosexually married man who rapes and abuses his wife is committing horrific evil that is in no way mitigated by the fact that it is heterosexual. God forbid that anyone might suggest otherwise.

We do have a biblical model based on excusing yourself from repentance on the grounds of comparative sin. It is found in Luke 18, in the parable of the Pharisee and the Publican, and it doesn't go so well for the Pharisee:

> 10 *"Two men went up into the temple to pray, one a Pharisee and the other a tax collector.*
> 11 *The Pharisee stood and was praying this to himself: 'God, I thank You that I am not like other people: swindlers, unjust, adulterers, or even like this tax collector.*
> 12 *I fast twice a week; I pay tithes of all that I get.'*
> 13 *But the tax collector, standing some distance away, was even unwilling to lift up his eyes to heaven, but was beating his breast, saying, 'God, be merciful to me, the sinner!'"*

The paradigm of comparative sin proves to be a boat with holes, as the sins of self-righteous Pharisees reveal themselves more often than not to be more heinous than the sins of humble Publicans. This is true, even if the Pharisees sin in their heterosexual lust and the Publicans sin in their unwanted homosexual lust.

The practice of sexual sin is a fruit of other, more devastating sins: pride and lust. Satan loves best those Christians who delude themselves with fantasies of excused fleshly grandeur, but then walk the road to hell with misapplied confidence. Hannon says that this presumption that heterosexual sexual orientation is sanctified simply because it is heterosexual "ushers in a pathetically uncritical and...unmerited self-assurance, not to mention an inaccurate measure for evaluating temptation."[11] I agree.

But we still must confront what the Bible says about the "unnaturalness" of homosexual sex in Romans 1:

> 25 *For they exchanged the truth of God for a lie, and worshipped and served the creature rather than the Creator...*

26 For this reason God gave them over to degrading passions; for their women exchanged the natural function for that which is unnatural,
27 and in the same way also the men abandoned the natural function of the woman and burned in their desire toward one another, men with men committing indecent acts and receiving in their own persons the due penalty of their error.

Romans 1 will always hold a powerful place in my life as a believer. I first read these words when I was in a committed lesbian relationship. My first response was to ridicule them. I had not always identified as a lesbian, but once I met my first lesbian lover, I was hooked. I was sure I had found my real self. And I was mighty sure that I knew myself better than this ancient book whose words called into question my ability to discern right from wrong.

But after working through the rest of the Bible multiple times, I had to confront that the God who created us has the right to define those "ordinances" of his creation,[12] including human sexuality. While I came to believe that by God's design, sexuality is for the fulfillment of God's creation ordinance, I did not experience this truth. I only embraced God's truth because my conscience condemned me. At a certain point, I realized that the Bible was God's Word, and it had the right to condemn me, and not the other way around.

Through God's power, I embraced the Bible, as I do any number of things about God and faith that in my sin or limitation I don't experience firsthand. And because I embraced it, as a new believer who still felt very much like I lived experientially on the wrong side of the natural revelation tracks, I had to study the idea of biblical sexuality from two perspectives: 1) biblical ethics (what the Bible declares), and 2) personal growth in Christ. Personal growth in Christ flowed from the pastoral care given by Pastor Ken Smith and other members of the Syracuse Reformed Presbyterian Church, and it flowed through the means of grace that lead us, in spite of our feelings or past behavior, to live as new creatures in Christ, standing in the risen Christ alone. It occurred

Natural law — the moral revelation that God gives in creation.

to me early in this journey that to declare the biblical ethics of *natural law* scriptural is not necessarily implying that its point of view is always pastoral.

Natural Revelation as Biblical Ethics

Romans 1:18–20 puts forth the biblical idea of what theologians call "natural revelation" — the disclosure of God and his laws as they are seen in nature. Romans 1 says this:

> *18 For the wrath of God is revealed from heaven against all ungodliness and unrighteousness of men who suppress the truth in unrighteousness,*
> *19 because that which is known about God is evident within them; for God made it evident to them.*
> *20 For since the creation of the world His invisible attributes, His eternal power and divine nature, have been clearly seen, being understood through what has been made, so that they are without excuse.*

Let me tell you straight up that these words drove me mad. I hate to think in terms of wrath, punishment, and the expectation that we all learn the same lessons from the same perceptions or experiences. Every fiber in my postmodern being retaliated against this way of thinking. But here we see that God holds us responsible for "suppress[ing] the truth in unrighteousness" (v. 18). He declares that ungodliness is "evident within them" (v. 19). He portrays man as "without excuse," because his power and character have "been clearly seen" and "understood through what has been made" (v. 20).

When I read this as an unbeliever, I found this patronizingly insulting. I loved my lesbian partners and the community that we created, and yet these verses made it evident that God wanted me to behave differently than I did. Only later as a believer could I see why this argument did not convince me: God does not claim that the gospel is found within this portrayal of his power and divinity in nature. In other words, "natural revelation" exposed my sin, but God understood that there is a difference between the diagnosis and the cure. Natural revelation portrays God's diagnosis, but only in the gospel do I find the cure. That seemed fair. It seemed to be saying that my responsibility as an image bearer required that I know more of God than that which is found in the law. Specifically, it goaded me to know the gospel, to study it, to ponder it, to allow it to creep through the wall that I had built around my heart. Natural revelation revealed my sin and caused me to doubt the unitarian message that sin did not matter. This burgeoning awareness reminded me of one of my favorite dead white guys.

Thomas Aquinas (1225–1274 AD) believed that natural law led to natural moral awareness. Thomas Aquinas read Aristotle (384–322 BC) through a Christian lens in the same way that St. Augustine (354–430 AD) read Plato (c. 422–347 BC). I found Aquinas to be one of the best minds that ever walked the earth, and I was troubled to arrive at a conclusion that he did not. But I also knew enough about my own sins to know that some held more surface interests, while others really pulled at my heart. Sexual sin ran deep and hard for me. I needed a whole lot more than moral awareness, and I knew it, even if those around me didn't.

But I had bigger problems than those posed by squaring off with a dead white guy, even one for whom I felt affection. Every time I heard a Christian in my church declare natural law as the trump card to end the problem of homosexual sex, I just wanted to scream. Do you have any idea how many times people have told me that the Bible made Adam for Eve, not Adam for Steve? If I had a nickel for each time, I would be a millionaire! I could not understand why people in my church were so convinced by this argument. Adam and Steve did not rock my boat in the least bit.

Natural law is effective biblical ethics and public policy, but it is an incomplete pastoral instrument, because natural law is not the gospel. When we preach the gospel, we preach the promise of a new life, new mind, new hope, new purpose, new union with Christ, new company of the Holy Spirit, new pardon of sin, new affinity for repentance and closeness with God, new love of the law, new ability to obey, new understanding of why God demands chastity outside of marriage and fidelity inside of marriage, new patience with people who do not yet know Jesus, new perspectives on suffering and affliction, addiction and change, new hatred of our own sin and patience with the sin of others, new responsibilities, new heartaches, new friendships, a new family from within the body of Christ, new allegiances, new dangers, and new grace. I needed the expulsive love of my risen Savior to whisper in my ear that my burgeoning conviction of sin was truer than what my flesh craved.

Through the power of the gospel, it became clear that God's provision of salvation required that I understand from his point of view a biblical sexual ethic. Because God in Jesus Christ was my Savior and friend, I realized that I needed to take the time to really get to know him. I needed to steep myself in the means of grace and wean myself from the world. And God used natural revelation to reveal my sin in this way: my knee-jerk response to creation ordinances revealed to me that I was resistant to know God. And that was sin. So I committed myself to study these ordinances. It became clear that marriage between a man and a woman was by God's design. It also seemed clear that God did not design everyone for marriage. Natural revelation told me what God required, but without gospel grace, I could no more live out these Christian ethics than I could walk on water.

Gag Reflex and the Problem of Point of View

Does the fact that homosexual sex is, according to the Bible, against nature mean that a useful Christian response to this is the gag reflex? Does it logically follow that if you are on the right side of God's story, you should gag (i.e., become visibly sick to the point of wanting to vomit) at the sin of others?

This makes sense in one way only: we are called to have a conscience that is sensitive to recognize sin and a Christian reflex that is quick to flee from it. But there is a serious problem with the gag reflex: it allows for a voyeuristic approach to sin. The gag reflex argument describes gay sex in unnecessary detail, unwittingly encouraging Christians to dwell on these sins to the harm and detriment of all of us. The sexual orientation paradigm has turned people into practices, thus making the gag reflex a condemnation of people themselves, not only people who engage in such practices, but also people who desire them.

While likely unintended, three things happen when Christians write blogs or books and paint a gay sex scene as an encouragement to gag:

1) The Christian writer scapegoats faithful Christians who love Jesus and yet struggle with unwanted homosexual lust. Indeed, these faithful and struggling Christians become the example of the person who should cause you to want to gag or vomit. And, likely, they are sitting in the pew next to you every Lord's Day morning.

2) The Christian writer portrays sex acts with vivid recall that will unwittingly entice some Christians to desire it or bring to mind the repented sin of years gone by, causing grief and anguish and a general reliving of the very things that Jesus has covered with his blood.

3) The Christian writer gives ammunition to people who have exclusively heterosexual desires to unmerited self-righteousness, creating a sexual identity that is potentially marked by the deadly sin of pride. Indeed, this "gag reflex" that some evangelicals endorse reveals that the concept of sexual orientation weakened biblical sexuality for everyone by allowing heterosexually expressed sexual sin to pass under the radar as tolerable because they somehow reflect the biblical norm (including pornography and adultery), and by exposing homosexually expressed sexual sin as the only one of great moral danger.

In sum, sexual orientation is harmful for self-identified heterosexuals because it bathes heterosexual sexual desire with sanctifying impulse—even that which is directed outside of marriage, through pornography and adultery—and demonizes homosexual desires as unnatural—failing to register that what renders sexual orientation unnatural is the neologism itself. When Romans 1:26 references *unnatural* ("exchanged the natural function for that which is unnatural"), it regards practice, not personhood; it references what a person ought not *do* (morally), not who a person *is* (ontologically). Any believer who has been justified by God is ontologically a child of God, a son or daughter of the King, and set apart from before the foundations of the world. There is no ontological category of sexual orientation. The idea of identity emerging from sexual desire embodies a philosophy of the soul that is false. Sexual orientation is a category that adds and stirs all solipsistic fallen sexual impulses and desires into a paradigm of individual entitlement, writing off God's covenantal relationship to his people and his teleological design of sexuality within biblical marriage, and denying that their fruit rests in redemption through Christ's blood alone.

Christians who feel beholden by the culture to use the concept of sexual orientation ought to stop and ask one question: where ought we to situate sexual orientation in relation to biblical principles? If we were to fish around for a biblical place to contain this neologism (which is sloppy theology at best), it could only be traced to the biblical concept of "flesh."

In the Bible, the concept of "flesh" is mainly used in three different ways: 1) to describe the human body (i.e., "flesh and blood"); 2) to describe human weakness and the perishable nature of the body (i.e., "all flesh is grass"); and 3) to describe the sinful nature of fallen man, as described in Romans 8:

> *6 For the mind set on the flesh is death, but the mind set on the Spirit is life and peace,*
> *7 because the mind set on the flesh is hostile toward God; for it does not subject itself to the law of God, for it is not even able to do so.*

Indeed, *The Westminster Larger Catechism* reminds us to "guard against the extremely common error that the word *flesh* means a part of our human nature. It does not refer to a "lower" nature; it refers to our whole nature as corrupted by sin."[13] Born in the sin of Adam as we all are, "there is nothing human that has not been corrupted and defiled by our fall into sin."[14] Thus, "sexual orientation," or any term that seeks to define humanity without recognizing our fallen nature, and the redemptive grace offered in Jesus Christ, can only misrepresent humanity in the long run, even if it appears to provide some temporary clarity for the here and now.

At its best, sexual orientation is a vestige of our flesh.

At its best, sexual orientation is a vestige of our flesh. The term itself cannot be labeled sin or grace. Sexual orientation fronts a category of personhood that privileges natural desires over redeemed ones. One's sexual orientation—heterosexual or homosexual or bisexual or pansexual (and the list will not end here)—cannot be sanctified, because sanctification would indeed cause its eradication, as sanctification obliterates all pretenses of the staying power of natural virtue or vice over and against the power of the gospel. And while you must repent of sexual sin, you cannot repent of sexual orientation, since sexual orientation is an artificial category built on a faulty premise. You have a better shot of putting Humpty Dumpty together again than reinventing sexual orientation as a biblical category.

Major doctrines of the Christian faith are at stake in this conversation. Sanctification is God's desire and his gift to all believers: "for this is the will of God, your sanctification; that is, that you abstain from sexual immorality" (1 Thess. 4:3). Therefore, there is no such thing as a believer who has been justified by God (pardoned by judicial decree) without also being sanctified (infused with God's grace that subdues sin and enables the believer to live in obedience). If there is truly no sanctification (including the sanctifying grace of humility that knows sin's power in our life and our need for Jesus because of this), there is no fruit of conversion.

In the language of *The Westminster Catechism*, justification is imputed (a legal term that changes a person's account and status before God). In contrast, sanctification is infused (literally, "poured in," describing the way that God pours into believers his love and grace such that the personal character, not the legal status, of the believer is changed by God). Sanctification is "an act of God's free grace; a work by which God infuses grace and power, a work in which God subdues sin, different in degree in different persons, incomplete and imperfect in this life, [and] a divinely planted and watered spiritual growth of Christian character."[15]

What is sanctified is the *believer*, not the believer in the context of his or her sexual orientation, the artificial category mistake spawned by Freud and inbred into every conversation about sexual identity that has trailed along after him ever since. If you are a child of God, washed in the blood of Christ, you should never again be defined by or reduced to an "orientation" linked to a pattern of even persistent temptations.

Personal Identity and Sexual Orientation

When I "came out" as a lesbian in 1992, I had already been living as one for a few years. The experience of coming out was for me a rite of passage, embarked upon in the hope of being honest and bringing the details — private and public — of my life together. Coming out as a lesbian was my way of staking my claim at identity. Somewhere between college and graduate school, in my mind, things shifted from "Why do I feel this way?" to "This is who I am: take it or leave it." But never did I use the concept of sexual orientation to describe my sexual identity. I was a nineteenth-century scholar and I held some scholarly suspicions about this category. Also, "sexual orientation" was not part of my lesbian, poststructural, queer culture.

Coming out, naming my experience, and claiming my personal identity mattered enough to me to risk relationships and job opportunities. I thought long and hard about the ramifications of this disclosure. Terms like "same-sex attraction" were also not in my vocabulary. I had never heard of Exodus International, and I likely would have described an "ex-gay" as an unhappy camper. And no one in the LGBT community from which I emerged would have ever claimed to have been "born this way." We believed that sexuality was fluid. The "born this way" idea was potentially pathologizing to lesbians of my generation.

Because we were leaders in poststructural feminism and Queer Theory, disciplines that understood sexuality as a *social construct*, we situated ourselves—for good or bad, right or wrong—in the world of free choice. We claimed psychological proof that gender and sexuality were social constructs, and as such, matters of personal expression that can be changed, resisted, or shaped as our own individual sense of personal integrity and desire allowed. Because we believed that "gay is good," we embraced a missionary's zeal about political and social activism. We believed that all good things flowed from our sexual desires and the egalitarianism of our households.

> Social construct—a category created by society.

Adrienne Rich, the late feminist, lesbian, poet, essayist, and professor, gave words to my world in her essay, "Compulsory Heterosexuality and Lesbian Existence."[16] Her essay explained my feelings and personal experience in ways no one else had ever done before. I was amazed that there was a name for who I was. Like most lesbians of her generation, Adrienne Rich initially defined herself as heterosexual, was married to a man from 1953 to 1970 and bore children. She became widowed in 1970. Over time, her sexual attractions to one woman emerged. (Adrienne Rich and Michelle Cliff remained partnered until Rich's death at age eighty-three in 2012.) Rich introduced vocabulary into my world that helped me look in a mirror and recognize what I saw.

For Rich, all women exist on a *lesbian continuum*, where women-identified roles and experiences make up the fabric of life and the meaning of women's history. Importantly, this included nonsexual affections. The term itself, lesbian continuum, upended any "sexual orientation" idea or a God-ordained gender and sexual essentialism.[17] *Lesbian* became the new norm for all women. She wrote: "I have chosen to use the terms lesbian existence and lesbian continuum because the word 'lesbianism' has a clinical and limiting ring.... I mean the term lesbian continuum to include a range—through each woman's life and throughout history—of women-identified experience, not simply the fact that a woman has had or consciously desired genital sexual experience with another woman."[18] Thus, lesbian continuum became a map over time of both women who had sexual desires for other women and those who did not, but who wanted to excuse themselves from the history of patriarchy that, divorced from God's holy ordination, felt obligatory, compulsory, dangerous, and deadly.[19]

Why Words Matter

Because I am a new creature in Christ, my identity, and the words that I use to reflect that, must honor the primacy of Christ indwelling my life. It must. I died and rose again with Jesus, my Lord. For all who claim Christ, personal identity is a constant war between flesh and spirit, between the who-I-am-in-the-flesh and my new nature, redeemed, but still fallen. Much of this tension Paul captures in the book of Romans. Chapter 12 begins thus:

> 1 Therefore, I urge you, brethren, by the mercies of God, to
> present your bodies a living and holy sacrifice, acceptable to
> God, which is your spiritual service of worship.
> 2 And do not be conformed to this world, but be
> transformed by the renewing of your mind, so that you
> may prove what the will of God is, that which is good and
> acceptable and perfect.

We need to daily "renew our minds" and "present our bodies a living sacrifice," but we can only do this by the "mercies of God."

Because we labor for sanctification in both private devotions and in community, it is also important, vital, and lifegiving for others in your church to know, in fullness of truth, who you are. For this reason, it is important to me that Christians who struggle with unwanted homosexual desires feel safe and welcome in a church community, knowing that God's people will meet you in your struggle and stick by your side for the long haul. It is not, in any way, immodest or un-Christian to tell people who love you that you daily bear the weight of homosexual desire, and that this affects your current relationships and your legitimate fears about the future. If this is your experience, you need to share this so that people in your church community can be your friend in a real way. There is no shame in truth telling.

Truth telling is not the same thing as coming out.

But truth telling is not the same thing as coming out. Coming out refers to a right of passage in the gay community where you set yourselves apart from your family of origin. Christians *convert*, and in conversion, God gives you a new family in the church. Conversion means that a Christian's primary loyalty is to the body of Christ in its diversity, not a ghetto of like-minded believers who assemble an identity based in patterns—even fixed and pervasive ones—of temptation. Who could share the burdens of our hearts without the family of God to listen?

In one of those many passages of the Bible that brings me to tears, Jesus tells us something transformative about the family of God. In Mark 10, we read this:

> *28 Peter began to say to Him, "Behold, we have left everything and followed You."*
> *29 Jesus said, "Truly I say to you, there is no one who has left house or brothers or sisters or mother or father or children or farms, for My sake and for the gospel's sake,*
> *30 but that he will receive a hundred times as much now in the present age, houses and brothers and sisters and mothers and children and farms, along with persecutions; and in the age to come, eternal life."*

These verses promise that a brother or sister should never be or feel alone, isolated, unloved, or unwelcome. These verses tell us that through brotherhood and sisterhood, believers are to receive "a hundred times as much now in the present age." That does not mean that we abandon brothers and sisters to go it alone, but rather that we walk together shoulder to shoulder, as we look forward to eternity, where our inner renewal will be complete

111

and full. Together and in community we help each other to not lose heart, saying, with Paul, "Therefore we do not lose heart, but though our outer man is decaying, yet our inner man is being renewed day by day" (2 Cor. 4:16).

I long to see the church serving as this kind of community.

In the Christian community that Christ portrays here, our churches are intentionally diverse and we all call ourselves by the one name of greatest honor: Christian.

Self-Representation

What Does It Mean to Be *gay?*

What the Word *gay* Means

The word *gay* shifted from its historical sixteenth-century meaning of merry, bright, festive, and joyous, to a precise portraiture of male effeminacy in the eighteenth century, to a new kind of person in the nineteenth century, to a term affirming the inherent goodness of homosexuality in the twentieth century.

We associate the word *gay* with its twenty-first century dictionary meaning: a homosexual. Importantly, the term *gay* became associated with homosexuality at the same time that it became associated with homosexual liberation (freedom of oppression and stigma for being gay). The term was a contested one. Gay-detractors used it pejoratively, and gay-affirmers claimed it back. The *Oxford English Dictionary* (*OED*) traces word etymologies and meanings as they change over time, culture, and use. The *OED* shows how both the term *gay* and its political advocacy and affirmation of gay rights came into existence simultaneously.[1]

Later in the twentieth century, after the concept of homosexuality was rightly removed from the *Diagnostic and Statistical Manual* in 1973, the phrase "gay is good" became associated with the term, a maxim intended to shift social focus away from illness and pathology to the asserted necessity of sexual orientation as a human-defining and distinguishing term, one that heralds a new wave of diversity.

Homosexual practice is not the consequence of mental illness. That is not how the Bible records things. God declares homosexual practice a sin from which we must repent. But the concept of sexual orientation blurs the relationship between personhood and sexual practice (desired or actual). Christians are called "saints" in the Bible. We who bear Christ's spilled blood are a royal priesthood. Any category of personhood that reduces a saint to a sum total of his or her fallen sexual behavior is not a friend of Christ.

The word *gay* has a power and history that Christians who claim it as self-representation need to reckon with. When Christians embrace the moniker *gay*, we enter into the worldview that declares political advocacy, sexual affirmation, and the overriding philosophy that homosexual practice is good. This is in contrast with the biblical norms of fidelity within marriage and chastity outside of marriage. We can use words and words can use us. The meaning and interpretation of words in context of grammar and syntax transcend our good intentions.

Therefore, to the best of our ability to discern this, God's intent must trump ours when defining a word's semantic range. As Christian brothers and sisters, we affirm Christ in us and working through us by grace alone, not our patterns of temptations, special interests, or even our physical conditions. Our life in the flesh matters, but it is not the most important thing. We agree with Paul that our preference is to be "absent from the body and to be home with the Lord" (2 Cor. 5:8). The blood that ties us together and to our Savior and Friend trumps all.

Words, though, are unstable creatures. We need revised dictionaries each year because new words enter into the culture, and because words do change over time. In the 1990s, many people in the gay community (myself included) ditched the term gay or lesbian for the term *queer*. Why? In the sixteenth century, *queer* was an adjective and meant perverse, strange, bad, worthless, and counterfeit. By the eighteenth century, *queer* became dominantly used as a verb, and it meant to interfere with or spoil ("queer a pitch"), to swindle or to cheat. By the late nineteenth century, *queer* was a pejorative term used again as a noun to refer to a new kind of person, a homosexual.[2] In an effort to take back the word, queer activists embraced it in order to remake it on our own terms. We believed that signs (words) and signifiers (meanings) could be reshaped by sheer force of use, that they were inherently unstable and only found meaning in our usage of them. We believed in the social construction of gender and sexuality through language. We wanted to claim this term on our turf, because once it became our term, it lost its pejorative power.

So, if radical queer activists can play with language to redeem it, why can't evangelical Christians? If language has an inherent fluidity, why not use this on our own terms? Because as Christians, we need to practice what we want to model: a call to use words honestly. A call to use words honestly, in ways that correspond to God's truth. And, while words do have a semantic range of meaning, we are never to use this fact to deny that God's standard for obedience is the bulls-eye.

Words function in grammar and syntax. We need to not only consider their *semantic* range of meaning, but also their role in a sentence, that is, their meaning-making power. Andreas Köstenberger Semantic—relating to the meaning of words. puts it this way: "Just as every nation has laws to govern the life of its citizens, so every language has a system of grammar and syntax that stipulates proper rules and conventions of usage for that language."[3] Adjectives hold powerful laws in the English language, and adjectival modifiers serve to change the noun they modify. Indeed, the word *modify* means just that: "to limit, to change the form or external qualities of a thing; to shape, to give a new form of being to; to vary, to moderate, to qualify, to reduce in extent or degree."[4] A modifier limits and reduces the noun.

In the phrase "gay Christian," *gay* is a descriptive or limiting adjective, and its job is "to indicate the quality of a noun or pronoun."[5] It indicates what kind of Christian you are. When a limiting adjective is used to define a people group, it is a mark of identity. When you modify the noun *Christian* with the adjective *gay*, you pair terms with incompatible anthropologies, and recommend a false philosophy of the soul. Adjectival modifiers create new nouns. The case in point here is the category of "gay Christian," someone who both loves Jesus but is also, in attraction or action, persistently experiencing homosexual desires. The question is this: do we really want to say that gay Christians are a different type of Christian? Doesn't that create the kind of ghettoizing subgroup mentality that works against and not for real unity in Christ's Body?

Sometimes urgency creates the need to cut corners. If I feel my life is on the line, I will call out with an urgency that trumps all other rules of communication. Many people who identify as "gay Christian" are desperately trying to be heard. And the church needs to listen up, because the failure to listen degrades faithful brothers and sisters. The conservative Christian church bears some responsibility for driving brothers and sisters in Christ into this "gay Christian" ghetto with our blindness to the way that we have insensitively tried to fix or fix up all of the singles in our church.

In Christ, your self-representation is Christian.

When I question someone's use of the term "gay Christian," I am not saying that I do not want to hear about my sister and brother's deep feelings and longings. I am not minimizing these feelings and identities and senses of self. I am not discounting the heavy hand of loss that these feelings seem to portend, or the deep sensitivities and character building that marginalization ushers forth. I am saying that I want to be your friend. And, I'm saying that if you stand in the risen Christ alone, your self-representation is Christian.

So in the phrase "gay Christian," the noun *Christian* is changed by using a word whose sexual expression affirms behavior that stands apart from God's commands. In this way, it is different from a linguistic place keeper that identifies cultural affiliations (like Italian American, for example). "Gay Christian" differs from Italian American because God does not condemn national origin as a sin, but he has much to say about sex apart from the covenant of marriage, personal identity apart from Christ's exclusive claim, and self-representation that hijacks the appearance of sinful behavior and calls it grace. The word *gay* is only extricable from the sexual practice of homosexuality if you believe that sexual orientation is a morally neutral road map of humanity, and if it is a true measure of a man. Sexual orientation is no such animal.

It is not that adjectives can never modify the noun *Christian*, but they should do so in ways that neither create gratuitous factions[6] nor violate God's call that redeemed people identify themselves according to their new nature in Christ.[7] New nature does not necessarily mean new feelings (although it may). "New creature" is a term that beckons God's people to grow in Christ-likeness, to grow in sanctification, but we do harm to the call of Christ when we presume that opposite-sex desires should replace same-sex desires as the exclusive proof of real sanctification. "New creature in Christ" means that we have a new mind that governs the old feelings and a new hope that we are part of Christ's body.

Is "gay Christian" a term of identity, as I purport? Why can't it simply be a linguistic place keeper, one used to identify deep and abiding feelings that remain and even deepen over the years? A term that lets people know not to try to set you up with their unmarried cousins? Daniel Mattson quotes Chris Damian, who defends the use of the term *gay* as just one adjective among others. In his article,[8] Damian writes:

> I am a man; I am American; I am single; I am 5'10"; I am hungry; I am tired; I am happy; I am studious...and I am gay. I'm not just one of these things, but I am all of these things. You could ask me to not categorize myself in terms of my sexual identity because I am not just my sexuality; but if you're going to do that, you might as well not ask me to categorize myself at all.

Mattson says that Damian's argument that *gay* is just one adjective among many is disingenuous. He shows by example:

> Imagine a boy of fifteen. He wonders if he might be different than all of the other boys he knows. He often lies awake at

night, crying himself to sleep in anguish about it. He fears his parents might reject him if he tells them. Could God still love him, if it's true? And why would God allow this in this life anyway? He's depressed and doesn't know how he can survive and so he finally steels his resolve to tell his parents.

Mom and Dad, I don't know how to tell you this, so I'll just say it: I think I might be hungry.

We don't know much about the boy in Mattson's fictional story, but we do know that he is depressed and anxious and concerned because he knows God and God is speaking to his conscience. He is convicted in his conscience that he must not act on his feelings, and he does not know how to live with this. He feels that he has been dealt a harsh blow and he is fearful about his future.

Unbelievers would read this and say that the boy's only problem is that the world around him has stigmatized the word *gay*. But believers see the importance here of the church family coming alongside the boy and the boy's believing parents to help. Believers know that help comes not in destigmatizing the word *gay*, but in helping the boy and his family to do what all believers must do: mortify sin and live in faithfulness to God.

Gay is a term of identity.

No, *gay* is not just another adjective. It is a term of identity. *Gay* describes an intimate disclosure of real and abiding selfhood.

Words become culturally charged as identity markers when they stand for clusters of meaning, when their meaning changes from one cultural locator to the next, when their meaning arises out of political strife or liberation movements, and when they divide people according to political, social, or religious allegiance. Today, there is no keyword more explosively charged than *gay*. Raymond Williams in *Keywords: A Vocabulary of Culture and Society* situates words in "fields of meaning" because the "problem of meaning" is not resolved in either vocabulary, community, or culture.[9] This means that a word whose definition changes because of political unrest or social transformation is not one whose contemporary meaning is stable.

Words matter. Self-representation matters. And identity in Christ bleeds union in Christ and communion of the saints. This blood is truly life-giving. And the term "gay Christian" has great potential to mislead people, even as those who use it are seeking clarity, honesty, and transparency.

What Happens to Identity When *gay* Modifies Christian: Nothing? Everything?

Let's turn now to a Christian psychologist who supports Christians who identify as gay to be heard.

Mark Yarhouse, in *Understanding Sexual Identity: A Resource for Youth Ministry*, offers a pastoral guide to meeting people where they are. Speaking of the need to engage with people with "convicted civility," a delicate "balance between holding convictions as a Christian and communicating those convictions with civility,"[10] Yarhouse begins by defining his terms, and by distinguishing sexual identity from sexual orientation:

> Sexual identity refers to the act of "labeling" oneself based on one's sexual attractions or orientation. Common sexual-identity labels include gay, straight, lesbian, and bisexual. You may hear some kids refer to themselves as questioning, curious, or queer. Still others prefer not to adopt any label whatsoever. The difference between attractions and orientation is just a difference in the strength of those attractions and how persistent they are for a person.[11]

This is helpful. Affectional attractions are not sinful *per se*, because these attractions speak more to relational comfort or solidarity, and not necessarily to implied desire for sexual contact. But is this what most people mean when they talk about same-sex attraction (SSA)? In our sex-charged world, most people use SSA to refer to sexual attraction. When the word *attraction* goes

Continuum—progression of elements varying by minute degrees.

through the grist of culture, it implies a *continuum* of feeling, some affectional and some sexual. That is why the term SSA can be misleading.

But why *would* we subsume affection into the paradigm of sexuality? This is not a biblical understanding. Perhaps one purpose of the APA's use of the term "affection" and its separating it from sexual desire (represented in the hyphenated coordinating conjunction, "and/or") is to show the obvious: that not all people who experience homosexual desires are attracted sexually to every person of the same sex that they encounter. To those of us who have been part of an LGBT community, this is crystal clear and drop-dead obvious.

When I identified as a lesbian, I was never sexually desirous of each and every woman in my life. For example, I was part of a women's running team, and many women on my team also identified as lesbian. A small group of us trained together almost daily over a five-year period (and two Guinness World Records!). We were the best of friends, and even though we all identified as lesbian we were never romantically attached with one another. The APA's use of the term "affection" is meant, I believe, to help people understand this: that homosexual desire, even if consistent over time, is rarely indiscriminate.

But while the APA's definition of sexual orientation defends people with homosexual desires from the misunderstanding that renders same-sex sexual desire indiscriminate, the paradigm can also distort or confuse the category of human affection by subsuming it within the category of sexual.

Platonic—of a relationship marked by the absence of romance or sex.

When every relationship is potentially erotic, no relationship has the boundaries it needs. Maintaining a boundary around sexual behavior and making that the exclusive domain of the covenant of biblical marriage is necessary for platonic relationships to maintain their integrity as *platonic*. We have lost the ability to be nonsexually same-sex affectionate, and this is a costly human loss. But something else happens here: it confuses people about what is sin and what is not. Misplaced guilt is Satan's weapon. There is no sin in *homosociality*—an abiding preference to find your closest and most meaningful friendships with members of your own gender. Nor is homosociality "gay."

Yarhouse also distinguishes between nouns and adjectives, not in terms of their grammatical purpose (how words use us), but in terms of their contemporary communicative purpose (how we use words). Yarhouse writes:

> We need to distinguish between the noun (Gay) that refers to sexual identity and the adjective (gay) that refers to sexual orientation.... [I]n our culture today "gay" is used by nearly everyone (and certainly most of the youth in your youth group) to refer to a homosexual orientation. To use it to refer to identity only will be confusing to them.[12]

Yarhouse wants to make a clear distinction between sexual orientation and identity, but the line is not as distinct as he suggests. All acts of self-representation exist on a continuum, and a continuum allows for fluidity and overlap. We all have a deep need to know and be known, to let people know where we stand, with whom we stand, and where we hurt. I support this. But self-representation also embodies a sociological consequence, as self-representation has a community appeal to it. This community appeal means that others depend on who we say we are.

When we as Christians call others to come out as gay, as a desire to create community and to find role models, we are operating in the realm of identity, as identity situates you in time, place, and culture. To put it simply, you use words, and words use you. Both are true because grammar trumps good intentions. And like it or not, the Bible's categories for self-representation are binaries: you are either saved or you are lost. If you are saved, you are saved for God's glory and his righteousness. He made the categories, and you don't get to blur the boundaries. As painful as it may be, salvation stories are often "single stories,"[13] as lives and loves must be abandoned for the love of God. A

Christian is not someone who blends, retains, or attempts to "redeem" enslavement from which Christ's blood grants liberty, community, friendship, and belonging.

Yarhouse explains another value in embracing the term *gay*—it de-stigmatizes it:

> Another benefit to distinguishing between Gay as a sexual identity and gay as a sexual orientation is that it avoids stigmatizing the word "gay." Why does this matter? Because some Christians are finding it helpful to use gay as an adjective, as a way of describing and naming their experiences.[14]

With Yarhouse, I oppose invoking culture war mentality about homosexuality. It oversimplifies a complex issue and is violent, not only to Christians who experience unwanted homosexual desire, but also to the compassion of Christ and the witness of the church. But I do not believe that sexual orientation is a biblically neutral starting point for this discussion. Self-representation travels on a continuum, as words can describe or identify a sense of deep and abiding persistency (situated on the continua of self-representation and identity), and assert an allegiance (situated in community). And words carry different elements of stigma sometimes for biblical and pastoral reasons, not only prejudicial ones. *Gay* is a word that carries stigma because of God's moral prohibitions against homosexuality. God is jealous for sexual purity in conduct and identity, and God's people should be also. Stigma in the hands of God is replete in the Bible, for many issues.

Because the Bible is clear on the point that homosexual practice is a sin, and because *gay* is a synonym for the implied desire for or practice of homosexual sex, the stigma of this term is an act of God's love, because God uses it to convict his children of their brokenness. When the culture wars raise the banner on *gay*, stigma becomes oppression, I know. But we would do well to remember that stigma reveals the gospel itself as a narrative of offense, and we who claim Christ as our Lord all began as his enemies, and all perceived the stigma of this exclusion.

While Yarhouse supports adults in using the term *gay*, he discourages teens from calling themselves gay Christians. Instead, he recommends they use the term same-sex attraction, as teenage sexuality is fluid and definitive labels are harmful.[15] Yarhouse writes: "A teenage girl [should be encouraged to] describe what she *feels*—she has feelings for the same sex—rather than saying something about the kind of person she *is*." In contrast, "a homosexual orientation is a bit different from simply describing experiences and feelings" as it "can also be a further step toward making claims about one's identity." This is important because "a person's identity determines the choices he or she makes in life."[16]

I wonder, though, why this same wisdom isn't also applicable to all Christians who struggle with homosexual desires. Sexuality constantly interfaces with other issues, including hormones and environment. I wonder why it is not also useful for people whose primary identity is in Christ to maintain a linguistic priority that emphasizes their worth and dignity as a daughter or son of the King, first, and their sexual desires (persistent, even abiding ones) as secondary. Would this not provide better redemptive language while at the same time communicating the depth of this issue, allowing all to embrace the truth that God is sovereign even over our struggles?

The Bible is clear that all sex outside of biblical marriage is a sin. The Bible is also transparent that homosociality is not sinful. In addition, temptation is not a sin, but temptations to sin are never good. They are never from God. Therefore, patterns of temptation can never be sanctified. Sometimes they arise from our own sinful desires (James 1:14). Because of this, making an identity out of sin patterns is itself a sin, as it deadens the conscience by defending the flesh instead of disciplining the conscience for godliness.

Moving up the scale, homosexual or heterosexual lust is a sin—even the unintentional and persistent kind that springs up like a hiccup or a reflex. Like all continua, however, these terms are nuanced and require careful biblical scrutiny. And, men and women register these things differently, as men move more

Coterminous—
having the same
boundaries or
meaning

quickly to lust and women remain (often, but not always) more comfortably in the domain of affiliation and bonding. Somewhere in this continuum, we need to confront the facts that Original Sin describes a sense of self so primal that it is *coterminous* with consciousness, and that it levels the playing field for us all.

Is Sexual Sin a Moral Problem or Physical Problem?

Is sexual sin a moral problem? Or is sexual sin a physical problem?

The biblical concept of natural fallenness is displayed in John's gospel, chapter 9, when Jesus meets a man born blind. This man's disability became a source of confusion for the disciples. The disciples wonder whose sin caused this man's blindness: his, or his parents'? And Jesus explains that his blindness is not the result of sin, but the occasion of God's display of power. In John 9, we read,

> 1 As He passed by, He saw a man blind from birth.
> 2 And His disciples asked Him, "Rabbi, who sinned, this man or his parents, that he would be born blind?"
> 3 Jesus answered, "It was neither that this man sinned, nor his parents; but it was so that the works of God might be displayed in him."

Jesus then spat on the ground, made clay out of his saliva mixed with the dust, and applied this to the man's eyelids. Jesus instructed the man to wash in the water of Siloam, and when the man returned, his vision was restored completely. Because Jesus healed this man on the Sabbath, the Pharisees accused him of unholiness, of breaking the Sabbath. Jesus made the blind man see so that the watching world could behold the blindness of the Pharisees. For those who had eyes to see, this healing was distinctive proof that the Messiah had come. But restored sight did not solve the healed man's problems.

Indeed, after the Pharisees interrogated the man, and the man explained that Jesus had healed him, they excommunicated the man and his parents: "[The Pharisees] answered him, 'You were born entirely in sins, and are you teaching us?' So they put him out" (v. 34). Excommunication would likely have put this family into poverty, social shame, and personal crisis. This blind and now healed man exemplifies the paradigm of natural fallenness. Blindness, while a natural consequence of the fall, is not a moral issue. Natural disabilities have no need to be forgiven because they are not a sin. They are healed through medical care or supernatural intervention, or they remain in the life of a person until glory.

Sexuality can be fallen in both natural and moral ways. Intersexuality[17]—being born with both male and female genitalia, for example—is an example of natural fallenness manifesting itself in sexuality. Intersexuality is a medical condition. Likewise, environmental accidents that result in dismemberment of genitalia can also fall into the category of natural sexual fallenness.

Original Sin levels the playing field.

But homosexual lust or sexual practice is a moral issue, as is its heterosexual counterpart outside of biblical marriage. And sexual desire for someone of the same sex is just one of many vestiges of Original Sin. Original Sin distorts a person in the way that we are all distorted. It does not set apart someone struggling with unwanted homosexual lust as somehow more distorted, or inherently more broken. Original Sin causes the actual and indwelling sin. Original Sin levels the playing field. Original Sin posits what is true about all people as God declares in Genesis 6:5: "Then the LORD saw that the wickedness of man was great on the earth, and that every intent of the thoughts of his heart was only evil continually." We pray that the Lord would reveal how we have been distorted by Original Sin from our inheritance in Adam, and for the imputation of this sin nature.

Anyone who resists sexual lust through faith in Christ is a testimony of Christian faith and God's sanctifying grace poured into this believer. This is biblical fruit. The man or woman who does this is a hero of the faith. The Bible makes a distinction between willful or presumptuous sins and hidden or deeply buried sins, and this helps us make sense of sexual desire.[18] A willful sin is one you premeditate; a hidden one (including indwelling sin) takes you by surprise, as it rises up like a reflex or involuntary response, and often takes you captive, as it resides in you and not outside of you. God calls us to repent of both kinds of sin, although the former offers us a clearer sense of danger than the latter. Affection describes a state of being that is not sinful, while lust describes a desire for something that God says is sinful. These distinctions matter.

If the nineteenth-century neologism "sexual orientation" is not a useful place to begin our conversation about sexuality, where ought we to start? If I am diagnosed with cancer, I surely don't reject the word *cancer* or the diagnosis because I can't find the word in the Bible. But even if I go through a rigorous treatment of chemotherapy under the watchful eye of the world's most renowned medical doctor, as a Christian I know that healing comes from God's providential hand and that Jesus himself is the great physician; I know that this medically renowned doctor is God's means, and I thank God for that. And when we use terms whose contested definitions fall outside of a biblical world and life view, and when we ourselves serve as the diagnosing physician, we ought to take great comfort in the truth that God himself will not leave us nor forsake us.

Kent, my husband, is an avid student of church history. He often says that, in Western culture, there have been few attempts to actually eradicate the existence of the Bible. Instead, it just withers away with redefinitions of words, both biblical and common ones. It renders the Word of God no longer a substantial part of the armor of God, but merely a pacifier. My fear is that the use of the term *sexual orientation* when used as a morally neutral starting point for a conversation about biblical sexuality muddies the water about what Original Sin really means. It forgets that Original Sin is everyone's preexisting condition. There are moral realities embedded in the term *sexual orientation* for which Christians are called to account.

What Is a Biblical Sexual Identity?

Importantly, the first two chapters of the Bible lay out God's definition of sexuality.

In Genesis 1, the created purpose of Adam and Eve is to nurture the earth, to steward it, and to procreate. I believe that the Bible teaches that Adam and Eve are real, historical people, not literary characters. Genesis 1:28 says: "God blessed them; and God said to them, 'Be fruitful and multiply, and fill the earth and subdue it; and rule over the fish of the sea and over the birds of the sky and over every living thing that moves on the earth." God's investment in humanity is capacious and majestic. But God's investment in humanity reveals that men and women are both complementary and distinct.

In Genesis 2:23–24, God remedies Adam's isolation by making Eve and then separating Adam and Eve into a covenant family. About this supernatural event, Adam proclaims: "This is now bone of my bones, and flesh of my flesh; she shall be called Woman, because she was taken out of Man." Adam and Eve are similar in their nature, vocation, and soul, but they are different in their sexual distinctions. Only because of this difference can they come together as one flesh: "For this reason a man shall leave his father and his mother, and be joined to his wife; and they shall become one flesh" (Gen. 2:24). That this is not just some descriptive analysis of an ancient family, but rather a paradigm for sexuality, is portrayed in the expression "for this reason." Heterosexuality becomes the pattern of biblical sexuality: "for this reason, a man shall leave." He shall leave. Future tense.

Fast forward to today. This business of one flesh as found in heterosexual marriage is by God's design. The concept of "one flesh" is rooted not only in the physical reality of conjugal union, but in the potential to procreate. The Bible declares that Eve was suitable for Adam (Gen. 2:18), that it is God who makes marriage (Matt. 19:6), and that Jesus defended the exclusivity of marriage (Matt. 19:3–6). What makes a marriage, then, is God's design. I have known many lesbians who have monogamous, committed, and faithful relationships. But even when we add civil legalization of gay marriage to this apparent reflection of common grace, God does not recognize these unions as true because they are not by God's design.

Marriage by God's design intends procreation, reflection, and anticipation. In the words of *The Westminster Confession of Faith*, "Marriage was ordained for the mutual help of husband and wife; for the increase of mankind with a legitimate issue, and of the Church with a holy seed; and for the preventing of uncleanness."[19] Christian marriage also reflects something of God's nature. As image bearers of a holy God, man and woman complement one another in marriage. Biblical marriage anticipates Christ's representation on earth in his bride, the church, as seen in Ephesians 5:

> *28 So husbands ought also to love their own wives as their own bodies. He who loves his own wife loves himself;*
> *29 for no one ever hated his own flesh, but nourishes and cherishes it, just as Christ also does the church,*
> *30 because we are members of His body.*
> *31 For this reason, a man shall leave his father and mother and shall be joined to his wife, and the two shall become one flesh.*
> *32 This mystery is great; but I am speaking with reference to Christ and the church.*

The layered interdependence of this metaphor—Christ and the church as original, and Christian marriage as a reflection—lays out that God designs marriage for his glory and for his reflection on earth. Importantly, reflections are only valid when the original is present. Thus celebrating marriage for marriage's sake is not a Christian impulse, because marriage was never just about lifelong companionship.

People who are heterosexually married are not, by virtue of their marriage, more sanctified or more "whole" or more rooted in God's will than single Christians. Marriage is by God's design, but Paul reminds us that single Christians are more useful in building the church and the Christian hospitality community, because single Christians are not as beholden to domestic and therefore worldly matters. In a majestic celebration of the biblical importance of singleness, John Piper's sermon "Single in Christ: A Name Better than Sons and Daughters" stands as a shining treatise.[20] Piper ends his commanding sermon with four points:

1) That the family of God grows not by propagation through sexual intercourse, but by regeneration through faith in Christ;

2) That relationships in Christ are more permanent, and more precious, than relationships in families;

3) That marriage is temporary, and finally gives way to the relationship to which it was pointing all along: Christ and the church—the way a picture is no longer needed when you see face to face;

4) And that faithfulness to Christ defines the value of life; all other relationships get their final significance from this. No family relationship is ultimate; relationship to Christ is.

Piper's sermon points us to glory, where there is no earthly marriage, where our sanctification is complete, where we inhabit the new earth in complete redemption, and where we finally know how to love God and each other in fullness of truth.

What Psalm 139 Teaches Me about Identity

When I was a new believer, a friend of mine in the Syracuse RP Church was an artist. Her art studio was in the attic of her house, and her house was a block from mine. One cold autumn afternoon, when I was struggling under the weight of my new identity in Christ and the war that it was waging in my flesh and my sense of identity, she invited me up to her place of refuge—her art studio. She was a busy mother of five children, and I marveled that she had such a room in this small, hyper-functional house where four boys shared one bedroom, with wall-to-wall bunk beds sometimes barricading the door. So Virginia Woolf-like, this room of one's own, I thought. I walked up the creaky attic steps and followed her through an opening that more resembled a hatch in a boat than a door in a house.

There unfolded a refuge that perfectly reflected my friend

in aesthetics, substance, color, and messiness. The room smelled of paint and dust, and it was simultaneously drafty from the bad windows and hot from the space heater. She swept away chalk, pencils, and fiber, and motioned me to sit on this new clearing. "The Psalms are my refuge," she said.

Our identity is in finding refuge in God. Nothing more.

Our identity is in finding refuge in God. Nothing more. Your identity crisis is good, she seemed to be saying. She opened to Psalm 139. This is a psalm about you and me. The "me" in the psalm is me—and you. Believers. "The Psalms are the words of Christ," she said. "We as Christians step into a multilayered embrace from our triune God as we sing them."

So we sang. We sang the melody for the first measure, and then my friend took the alto part and I took the soprano. We sang the whole psalm. Pausing in rhythm of our breathing, and stopping to meditate silently, and then, without announcing anything, starting up again. Psalm 139 reads:

> 1 O Lord, You have searched me and known me.
> 2 You know when I sit down and when I rise up; You understand my thought from afar.
> 3 You scrutinize my path and my lying down, And are intimately acquainted with all my ways.
> 4 Even before there is a word on my tongue, Behold, O Lord, You know it all.
> 5 You have enclosed me behind and before, And laid your hand upon me.
> 6 Such knowledge is too wonderful for me; It is too high. I cannot attain it.

The verb phrases here are powerful. God has searched me, he knows me, he understands me, he is intimately acquainted with me, he anticipates my words and self-diagnosis, and he puts hedges of protection around me. His knowledge of me is "too high. I cannot attain it."

7 Where can I go from Your Spirit? Or where can I flee from your presence?
8 If I ascend to heaven, You are there; If I make my bed in Sheol, behold, You are there.
9 If I take the wings of the dawn, If I dwell in the remotest part of the sea,
10 Even there Your hand will lead me, And Your right hand will lay hold of me.
11 If I say, "Surely the darkness will overwhelm me, And the light around me will be as night,"
12 Even the darkness is not dark to You, And the night is as bright as the day. Darkness and light are alike to You.

God's Spirit is omniscient. He rules all dominions, including hell itself. And because of this, when our sexual desires make us feel as though we "dwell in the remotest part of the sea," and that "darkness will overwhelm me," God tells us that if we make our home (including our identity) with him, he will guide us safely, because to him, darkness does not disable.

Importantly, God does not say that darkness will not terrify me or that if we find others who share our feelings, we will at least dwell in the remotest part of the sea with company. No. He tells us to come to him. Jesus echoes this when he beckons: "Come to Me, all who are weary and heavy-laden, and I will give you rest. Take My yoke upon you and learn from Me, for I am gentle and humble in heart, and you will find rest for your souls. For My yoke is easy and My burden is light" (Matt. 11:28–30). Psalm 139 continues:

13 For You formed my inward parts; You wove me in my mother's womb.
14 I will give thanks to You, for I am fearfully and wonderfully made; Wonderful are your works, And my soul knows it very well.
15 My frame was not hidden from You, When I was made in secret, And skillfully wrought in the depths of the earth;

*16 Your eyes have seen my unformed substance; And in Your
book were all written The days that were ordained for me,
When as yet there were not one of them.*

God is with us both in the remotest part of the sea and from
before the foundations of the world, when our substance was
unformed, but our destiny fully displayed before our Maker.
He formed our most intimate substance, and we are to give him
thanks, for each one of his children is "fearfully and wonderfully
made."

*17 How precious are Your thoughts to me, O God! How
vast is the sum of them!
18 If I should count them, they would outnumber the sand.
When I awake, I am still with You.*

As we dwell on God's nature (and by implication, a foreign
nature, not our own), our paradigm shifts. Because we are frail and
he is not, and because he is for us, our hope lifts. Question 4 of *The
Westminster Shorter Catechism* is one whose answer I dwell on
when I sing Psalm 139. In answering the question, "What is God?"
it declares: "God is a Spirit, infinite, eternal, and unchangeable, in
his being, wisdom, power, holiness, justice, goodness, and truth."[21]
When I ponder these words of the catechism, I am sitting under
the wisdom of the great cloud of witnesses, and participating in
a multi-historical communion of the saints. I am, in all of my
doubts, fears, and brokenness, surrounded by help.

*19 O that you would slay the wicked, O God; Depart from
me, therefore, men of bloodshed.
20 For they speak against you wickedly, And Your enemies
take your name in vain;
21 Do I not hate those who hate You, O LORD? And do I
not loathe those who rise up against You?
22 I hate them with the utmost hatred; They have become
my enemies.*

These are hard words, as they show that not all enemies will be reconciled through true repentance in Christian friendship. These words model that Christians are at times called to break allegiances with people.

As I write these words, Christians around the world are praying for the breakdown of wicked forces who have become killing machines and regimes in the Middle East. A friend last night at prayer meeting talked about viewing a YouTube video that displayed a brutal beheading, and how he wished he had not viewed that video, as the images of the murder scene haunt him day and night.

Our tendency is to find others who sin like we do.

I understand how he feels. All sin against God, all wickedness, finds its ultimate end in murder. Therefore, our loyalty must be to God, and it must go so deep that we own God's attitude about sin, especially when it comes to dealing with our own sin. Our tendency is to find others who sin just like we do, so that we won't be alone. We search for role models, so that we might minimize the sinfulness of our sin. We enlist others to help us in calling our sin a sanctifying grace. But we ought to quake in fear when we we find ourselves traveling that path. Because without intending it, such "covering" of sin renders us enemies of God, and not friends.

> 23 Search me, O God, and know my heart; Try me and
> know my anxious thoughts;
> 24 And see if there be any hurtful way in me, And lead me
> in the everlasting way.

God must search us to unearth our buried motives and providential prospects. We cannot search ourselves using the wisdom of the world. Self-knowlege is God's handiwork. And, when God exposes sin, he does this to call us to repentance unto life, such that the path to the "everlasting way" is rendered clear. This is God's promise to all. The "whole" Christian, in matters of faith and repentance, must come to God alone and on God's terms. This psalm gives me great comfort, as it helps me hand over the reins to God in all matters of identity and fear.

Do Christians, the Church, or the Witness of Christ Benefit from Asserting Sexual Identities Apart from Biblical Marriage?

Do we see anything in the Bible about compatibility, sexual orientation, gender identity, mixed-orientation marriages, and so forth? Is the Bible silent about these things? Hardly. The Bible is replete with examples of human diversity, including experiences felt and lived by sexual minorities. What does this say about all of us, in all of our brokenness and frailty?

Sam Allberry says it best: "Desires for things God has forbidden are a reflection of how sin has distorted me, not how God has made me."[22] So while marriage is by God's design, God does not design every person for marriage. And that is because he needs single men and women to be on the front lines of ministry. But that does not mean that their biblically married friends abandon them on the front line alone.

As all Christians attempt to discern matters of sin and grace and work together to give God glory in all of the details of our lives, I fear that our current language (i.e., sexual orientation, mixed-orientation marriage, gay Christian) is creating its own Tower of Babel in our churches. God created men and women so that we would enjoy him forever (eternally) and so that we would give him glory (on earth and in heaven). But when we even unwittingly create subcategories of Christians based in patterns of sexual sin, we are in effect taking aim at the very God who will safely hedge us in as we feel lost in the depth of the sea, as Psalm 139 outlines.

When we create subcategories of Christians to minimize the power of sin to seduce, we no longer share the same refuge that God promises in the Psalms, and the identity as refuge-takers that God offers. This becomes a problem not just for the individual Christian, who struggles to see God's love in the reality of his or her brokenness, but also for the Christian community at large and the visible church. As Richard Baxter put it long ago:

It is almost incredible how much ground the devil takes when he has once made sin a matter of controversy: some are of one mind, and some of another; you are of one opinion, and I am of another. If it were ever a controversy whether drunkenness, sexual promiscuity, swearing, stealing, or any villainy were a sin or not, it would be committed more commonly and with much less regret of conscience. By this means, good men themselves are dangerously disabled to resist sin, and are more prepared to commit it. Take heed lest the devil cast you into this sleep of carnal security.[23]

Our choice of vocabulary is no small thing. It may very well be the life jacket that keeps you afloat in this "sleep of carnal security" that we call the new normal. So, what ought we to do?

Christian love that is stronger than the lines that divide believers is the only response. I propose that we develop and maintain real Christian love for all believers, especially people who think differently than we do.

We need to make a committed effort to live out 2 Corinthians 13:11: "Be made complete, be comforted, be like-minded, live in peace; and the God of love and peace will be with you." This stands in direct contradiction to the spirit of contention. Avoiding strife and contention was so important to the great Jonathan Edwards, the eighteenth-century American theologian, that his famous "Farewell Sermon" to his congregation ended with these words:

> However wrong you may think others have been, maintain with great diligence and watchfulness a Christian meekness and gentleness of spirit; and labor, in this respect, to excel those who are of a contrary part.... And never think you behave yourselves as becomes Christians, except when you sincerely, sensibly, and fervently love all men, of whatever party or opinion, and whether friendly or unkind, just or injurious, to you or your friends, or to the cause and kingdom of Christ.[24]

Peace does not come naturally. Peace must be pursued.

Conflict

When Sisters Disagree

When Christians are divided on key issues, we must stop and listen. Because we agree that God's glory is the ultimate end of all things, we know all who are washed clean in the blood of Christ are on the same team. We therefore ought to stop and make sure that we are really listening to each other. Not the "yes, but" listening that pounces on every point of contention. But listening with empathy. To bring our conversation about sexual identity and union with Christ to a more personal level, I want to introduce you to a friend who uses the self-representation "gay Christian."

One thing to do when we are at an impasse with another Christian is to shut our mouths and give our Christian sister our full attention. I am grateful for my friend Rebecca and for her willingness to write this email to me (and to allow me to share our dialogue with you). This represents one email of many that we have exchanged over the past two years. You see, we are sisters in the Lord, but we disagree. And we are friends, and we disagree. Rebecca wrote this email out of love, and I share it out of love. Please hear my friend.

Since I was six years old and asked Jesus to fill me and guide my life, no other identity has meant more to me than the one I have in Christ. When I say I am gay, I am not taking on an identity. Nor do I have any desire to make my sexual orientation my identity. For me, saying I am gay is about being honest: I am attracted to other women. I didn't choose that. But it's real and it has significantly affected my life. Naming my reality is crucial. When things have no words, they remain confused and chaotic. Naming helps us to make sense of the world so we can live in it. In terms of language theory, language provides order. It's like the person who has an ailment who goes from doctor to doctor desperately trying to figure out what is wrong and is finally relieved when the condition can be named. For me the word *gay* is no different than saying "I am deaf" or "I am quadriplegic." It simply refers to the truth that I have an enduring affliction (whether based in biology or environment) that has not been healed despite many years of prayers. Some conditions are not healed this side of heaven. Like Paul, sometimes God allows a thorn to remain for his purposes.

Over the past twenty years I have wrestled with this question of how to be truthful about my reality. For a while I chose to say "I have same-sex attraction." I was part of the ex-gay movement at the time and using the term *gay* was frowned upon. We were encouraged to make contradictory and deceptive statements like, "I am not gay; I just have same-sex attraction." But I saw the tragic effects of that deception firsthand. I witnessed people rush prematurely into heterosexual marriages believing they were no longer gay. I saw leaders in the movement leave their spouses after ten or twenty years when the promised heterosexuality never transpired. And I have seen far too many return to same-sex relationships after years of celibacy, having become disillusioned that they were, in fact, still gay. Conservative Christians capitalized on this deception too. They took these ex-gay testimonies of "I am not gay" as literally true. Court arguments against same-sex marriage and other legislation have been made on the basis of alleged change in sexual orientation. I am not saying no one changes their sexual orientation, but it's much more complicated than many conservatives have been willing to admit. I have seen the marriages of some of these Religious Right poster children crash and burn to the ground under the weight of the deception "I am not gay."

In the past, *gay* meant an identity closely associated with the rise of LGBT rights. But a lot has changed in the last fifteen years. In today's lexicon, *gay* no longer means an identity. Most people under the age of thirty associate the term, not with identity or behavior, but with attraction. Merriam-Webster.com defines *gay* as "sexually attracted to someone who is the same sex." Dictionary.com has "of, pertaining to, or exhibiting sexual desire or behavior directed toward a person or persons of one's own sex; homosexual." The conservative Christian world is one of the only places where *gay* still means primarily an identity associated with a sociopolitical community. The problem that develops when Christians use privatized language to define terms in contradiction to common lexical use is the risk of appearing as liars. We know what we mean by our terms, but non-Christians don't. So when we say "I am not gay" but in truth we still have same-sex attraction, we come across as frauds. We defame the cause of Christ by the appearance of deception.

Any Christian who objects to the use of the term *gay* need thoughtfully reckon with these legitimate concerns and propose alternatives that avoid the pitfalls of deception. It will not do to resort to theological abstractions about Original Sin or pat answers about sexual orientation change. The church needs to let go of its defensiveness and ask itself these questions: How do we help a young person come to grips with a potentially lifelong condition so that hope deferred doesn't lead to disillusionment and abandonment of the faith? How do we help couples in mixed orientation marriages hold on to their marriages? What do we need to do to make lifelong celibacy a viable option in our culture for those who face that reality? How can we think cross-culturally and missionally with non-Christians who easily misinterpret our theological jargon so we don't harm the cause of Christ?

I stand in solidarity with Rebecca on many key issues, and I am enlightened by her life journey. I share her desire for truthful self-representation, and acknowledge that sexuality rests on a continuum, ranging between fixedness and fluidity. Christopher Yuan often says it this way: God is able, but not obligated, to give you what you ask for. I heartily agree. Sexuality is not a choice (although sexual activity is). Nor is it a lifestyle—something that you put on and off with ease. I believe Rebecca when she says that sexuality is not for her an identity: that her full identity is in Christ. Rebecca and I agree that sanctification is not coterminous with heterosexuality.

Is my own experience clouding my ability to hear Rebecca's, because, for me, my lesbianism was both an identity and sexual practice, and the scholarship that organized my life at the time corroborated this? Probably. My community and I valued and lived something called "identity politics."[1] But that is not Rebecca's reality. Rebecca leaves us with this question: "The church needs to let go of its defensiveness and ask itself: How do we help a young person come to grips with a potentially lifelong condition so that hope deferred doesn't lead to disillusionment and abandonment of the faith?" Although friends and prayer partners (we have never left a phone call without praying together), do Rebecca and I talk past each other, our different life experiences framing what we say and hear? Yes.

Share real life together in real time.

Rebecca asks me how do we help a young person (or old person) struggling with homosexual desires? My answer is to come to the table together. Stand side by side. Share real life together in real time. We do the same thing we would do with any other sister or brother, any other image bearer, and any other soul. We open our hearts and our homes. We open the

Word. We answer the phone at midnight, and we interrupt in a permanent, consistent, and organic way seasons of loneliness for our friend. We find out where the hard places are and bring in comfort. And we keep an eagle eye on our own prejudices and assumptions, our privileges and our blind spots. We stop telling people that their problems are not big. We don't flatten the terrain of unwanted homosexual desire by using analogies that may not fit. For example, we must stop claiming that the singleness experienced by people with unwanted homosexual desires is just like heterosexual singleness. For some, this may be so. But for others, the unique fingerprint of pain and loneliness conjured by unwanted homosexual desire is brought to a place of agony by such comparisons. In other words, we listen and we create real and regular friendship.

Rebecca is sharing her heart and also her experience in the "ex-gay" movement. This culture was shaped in part by theories rooted in Reparative Therapy[2] and its claim that homosexuality is the result of experiences (trauma, bad parenting, sexual abuse) and its solution is heterosexuality. It often encouraged a "prosperity gospel" approach to sexual healing and exaggerated success rates in "conversion" from homosexual attraction to heterosexual attraction—according to Rebecca and many others who have been eye witnesses to such deception—setting this shift into heterosexuality as its most treasured goal, and bypassing the importance of glorifying Christ in our struggle. Reparative Therapy programs often made promises they couldn't deliver, and broke the hearts and faith of many of their followers. God loves his people in our brokenness, and saved us when we were dead. If God was sovereign over the fall of humanity, is it so hard to imagine that he is sovereign over our fallen nature as well, in all of its manifestations and details, including for some people persistent unwanted homosexual desire? The issue here is saving faith.

Rebecca is my sister and my friend. I want to come up alongside of her—and have her come up alongside of me—and put this before the Lord, as we walk in faith and obedience. It is impossible to deal with the humiliating details of our lives while the logs in the eyes of others are clobbering around like drunken drivers. I imagine that this problem posed by clobbering logs is a little how it feels when I ask Rebecca not to use the word *gay* to refer to her sexuality.

Terms of self-representation can be honest declarations. But language emerges from different philosophical and theological commitments. When I say that Original Sin explains that we are all born this way, I am not intending a "theological abstraction" or suggesting that some people don't have heavier crosses to carry than others. Because of our fallen nature, sin is a sharp nail stuck in the flesh of our earliest consciousness, wedged in there from before the foundations of the world. For some people, that imprint of Original Sin takes the form of unwanted homosexual desires. Even after regeneration by the Holy Spirit, our sanctification can be slower than we want.

> To me, Original Sin is a democratizing idea.

In Christ, though, sanctification is a gift from God, not a willful act. If we live in the means of grace, then the pace of sanctification is God's blessing, and we should not disparage God's good gift by seeing it as paltry. So to me, the fact that our primal sins are also original to our consciousness is not meant as an assault or a minimizing of their power and presence. To me, Original Sin is a democratizing idea.

Rebecca refers to her sexuality as an enduring affliction, in part because Rebecca is committed to chastity and, unlike what I had done, Rebecca does not act on a sexual desire that dishonors God. But even enduring afflictions come to us from the fall, rendering neither "biology" nor "environment" neutral, sinless realities. She asks us to see that there is diversity among people who struggle with homosexuality. Rebecca says that for some, same-sex attraction is natural fallenness, while for others, it is moral fallenness. She asserts that if homosexuality is the consequence of moral fallenness—as it was for me—we would expect it to diminish in the sanctification process as we grow in the fruit of the Spirit. But I do not read sanctification in the light of a dramatic change of feelings, but rather, in the heart change that lives sacrificially for Christ in obedience to his will, in spite of feelings that run counter to God's command.

Rebecca stands in a different place than I did. She is devout and godly, and shares with us that she has experienced little change in her homosexual desires even as she has grown in the fruit of the Spirit and in sanctifying grace in other areas of her life. To me, her ability to exercise godly self-control over unwanted sexual desires is a shining example of sanctification. Rebecca concludes that the fallenness of her sexuality is like a physical disability. She reminds us that while God does promise growth in sanctification during this lifetime, God does not promise natural/physical healings.

Are we, Rebecca and I, disagreeing over words or more? And what ought we to do with this?

Have we broken fellowship, broken communion of the saints, with Christians who identify as gay because we can't get our vocabulary and the theology from which it emerges squared up at the get-go?

Can I walk side-by-side with my friend Rebecca even though we disagree on the use of the adjective *gay* for any Christian?

Yes.

Am I being politically correct?

No. I'm being biblically correct.

Can we open the Word together, pray together, and praise God as we are shattered? If not, why not? If Rebecca was my neighbor (and I'm praying for this), could we also worship together, bake bread, play cards with Kent and the children, serve meals at a shelter, share books, walk the dogs? I would like that.

Rebecca is my friend, but she is also a covenant child and a godly daughter of the King.

As Rebecca writes:

The conservative Christian world is one of the only places where *gay* still means primarily an identity associated with a sociopolitical community. The problem that develops when Christians use privatized language to define terms in contradiction to common lexical use is the risk of appearing as liars. We know what we mean by our terms, but non-Christians don't. So when we say "I am not gay" but in truth we still have same-sex attraction, we come across as frauds. We defame the cause of Christ by the appearance of deception.

We do not want to come across as frauds. We do not want to defame the cause of Christ by the sin of self-deception. I support my friend's right to accurate self-disclosure, to knowing and being known, to living in a Christian community where she is not daily or hourly assaulted by extra-biblical teaching about what a changed life in Christ looks like. I share with Rebecca the desire that when unbelievers overhear or engage Christians, we are people who speak with clarity and truth. I desire that laws of grammar and syntax, laws that we use to create communities of interpretative clarity, be honored. I support Rebecca in wanting to be known for how she struggles in the intimacy of her church community. I also hear Rebecca when she asserts that the under-thirty crowd interprets *gay* differently than I do. What we hear is important. What God intends is important, too.

Rebecca advocates for her right to name her experience, to be honest about her lived reality, and to not pretend that they are not what they really are. But she also puts forth a challenge, and not one that I can meet alone. If I don't like the term *gay*, what is a better form of self-representation?

I propose "living in chastity with unwanted homosexual desires." I propose this because it does not use a term that already has a secular political movement behind it, and because it makes clear that the one who bears it also strives to live by God's Word and his rules for sexual behavior.

Because I love Rebecca as my sister in the Lord, I see her standing in robes of righteousness, and I want her words to illuminate this status as a daughter of the King. And with all my heart, I believe that using *gay* to modify *Christian* dishonors God.

I understand that my alternative language also carries negative cultural baggage. But is it dishonest? Does it falsify your experience to say that you are someone who lives in chastity with unwanted homosexual desires? I am not trying to defend the ex-gay movement, but I too see a big difference between saying "I am gay" and saying "I am living with unwanted sexual desires." I need dialogue in real time on this. If my alternative language is unsatisfactory, then we need to work together on better language. In Christ, we are part of a body of believers, and therefore self-representation is a body issue. This takes time, friendship, and proximity. It takes community. Real community. Not blogs or "internet communities." This is a feet-on-the-floor and place-at-the-table problem. I'm game. I intend no violence when I ask you to use different language, language befitting the King's ransomed daughter. But I am asking nonetheless. I come in Christian love.

Our testimonies are not inspired; only the Word of God is. My testimony is neither representative nor proscriptive. And regeneration always renews the mind, even if our feelings remain unchanged to the degree that we want, and if our sanctification is slower than we expected. I realized through my new life in Christ's blood that the root of my lesbianism was the sin of pride—the pride that declared that my body would not be a commodity under male headship or patriarchy. Pride fueled sexual desires in me that exempted itself from men and directed itself to women. But the Word of God testified against my pride and the sexual desire that it ignited. I could not stand under the weight of its honor. After a radical conversion and the radical repentance it exacted, and after the wreckage of this, my lesbianism seemed like a case of mistaken identity, not an accurate self-representation. After conversion, my lesbianism revealed itself in a different hue than the one that Rebecca is facing, because sexuality is more complex than gay, straight, or bi. After conversion, life always looks different, as we have been humbled by a holy God and redeemed by the blood of our Friend and Savior, and comforted by the Holy Spirit.

I realize not everyone who embraces the term "gay Christian" will adopt the alternative language that I have proposed here. Not everyone will reject the word *gay* as an unhelpful and dangerous self-representation for the unified witness of Christ to a watching world. Conflict forces this issue and makes casualties out of friendships. So I will stand here: people are bigger (and more important than) the positions they take. This is my call to a new Christian ethics. Before we are fallen creatures, we are soul-infused ones, called to bear God's image in knowledge, righteousness, and holiness. And while our "flesh and blood cannot inherit the kingdom of God" (1 Cor. 15:50), when Jesus comes, and our bodies and souls are reunited, when we inherit a new earth, when we walk in complete sanctification in glory, we will know it: "the dead will be raised imperishable, and we will be changed" (1 Cor. 15:52). God's people all inherit this promise.

People are not their positions.

People are not their positions (or their problems). Our fallenness and the sinful nature that it bequeaths will not remain so in the new heaven we inherit after Jesus returns. I want to stand with Rebecca and walk in this Christian world together, continuing to pray, open the Word, repent of our sins, and seek God's guidance as we lock arms in Christian friendship. I want to share a place at the table with Rebecca. A complex friendship, to be sure, but I would not have it any other way.

What is my take-away hope for you as you read this? Friendship and neighborly proximity are necessary components to working through theological differences in Christian love. Ideas are not enough. Ideas buttressed with sarcasm and anger and thrust through the channels of the internet do more harm than good. Ideas have never been enough. Not for God. Ideas that divide must travel with warm pots of chicken soup when a friend is sick, and shoulder-to-shoulder gardening when the irises in one yard beg for thinning so that they can root in the next yard. Ideas that divide must travel on the back of Christian life practices that allow us to stand shoulder to shoulder as we submit before our holy and loving God. This is the Christian labor of real neighbors.

Community

Representing Christ to the World

S ome of the problems that I discuss in this book are insurmountable on their own terms. Grief, betrayal, loneliness, sin. How can any one person make meaningful inroads into problems that go so deep?

In the book of Hebrews, the writer tells us that reconciliation and restoration is done "by faith." The writer of the book of Hebrews declares, "Time will fail me if I tell of Gideon, Barak, Samson, Jephtha, of David and Samuel and the prophets, who by faith conquered kingdoms, performed acts of righteousness, obtained promises, shut the mouths of lions, quenched the power of fire, escaped the edge of the sword, from weakness were made strong" (Heb. 11:32-34)

The same is true today. We are conquerers of the problems that we face only by faith. And Christian hospitality and the community that develops from it is, I believe, the ground zero of our life in Christ: it is how our faith is visible and serviceable, powerful and potent. Hospitality from the home, in the neighborhood, and through the membership of the local congregation has the potential to transform us. Hospitality is our "by faith" bridge to each other, through Christ.

Hospitality in the Home Is Intentional

When I was in the LGBT community, someone's house was open every night, for food, fellowship, and advice. I presumed that that is how a community works: people have open availability with each other, and you are valued and remembered. A community is a place where others show concern if you do not show up to dinner, and celebrate when you start to turn the corner on that head cold.

In a community, when you return from a long trip and your plane lands, you send a one-word text message to someone who cares that you made it home safe. You text "safe" not because you need a ride home, but just because you are safe and home again. Your safety and the fact that you are home again matters to someone. "Safe" is all that you have to say. You don't need anything except for the most important thing: to know and be known.

When Christ captured my affections, he enriched each fiber of my life. I became a covenant member of my church. But I still found myself longing for more when it came to Christian community.

Community in my LGBT community was based in our shared identities and oppressions, and rested in sisterly trust because of the ways we were alike. But community for Christians rests not in our personal similarities, but in our shared futures: we are all bound to live as redeemed men and women, standing in Christ's righteousness, when he returns or when he takes us home.

Our similarities here and now do not sustain us.

Our similarities here and now do not sustain us. What matters is that we have made it home from a long journey, we are "safe," our sins forgiven, and while the cross we bear is heavy, we have the kind company of brothers and sisters that flows from union with Christ, and our eternal future is secure.

From the very beginning of our marriage, Kent and I have committed ourselves to hospitality. Because we recognize and cherish the important covenantal relationship of husband and wife, we see our marriage as an institution that has allowed us to minister hospitality in a unique way, using the blessing of marriage to create a home of hospitality that is inclusive and open.

Different seasons reflect this hospitality commitment differently: when we had just adopted a child, or had a new child in foster placement in our home, or when my aged mother lived with us, we practiced a different kind of hospitality. As Edith Schaeffer, wife of Francis Schaeffer and co-founder of the Swiss L'Abri Christian community, was fond of saying: doors have hinges. But when we have had a stable household (relatively speaking, of course), we have been able to have a more organic hospitality home, with one night designated for neighborhood ministry, the Lord's Day designated for our church family, and other days of the week open at meal times for what I like to call rhythm-of-life connections: meeting up with our church family in regular intervals so that we can share life.

In general, after school and work is done, our door is open, and our neighbors and their kids often trail in. Sometimes friends from church who work nearby stop over for a bite and a prayer. I set out extra plates. Because Kent and I both work from home, and because the kids are homeschooled, we are hungry for more than dinner when five o'clock rolls around, and we are supplied with great joy when we hear the door open and the dogs bark their greeting to someone Jesus has sent.

Over the years, I have come to learn that Christian community is built strong when we situate it on these two biblical principles: the paradigm of adoption and the fourth commandment (keep the Lord's Day holy). We must think about the principle behind hospitality, because Christian community must be intentionally crafted, with prayer and sacrifice. It doesn't just flow out of the day-to-day interests of the family. Sometimes we think that Genesis 1:28 covers the whole community thing: "and God said to them, 'Be fruitful and multiply, and fill the earth, and subdue it; and rule over the fish of the sea and over the birds of the sky and over every living thing that moves on the earth.'" God's giving of children to any marriage is a great blessing (and responsibility), but this verse speaks about how to steward what God has given you, not how to create or facilitate community.

Community renders enemies friends, and strangers brothers and sisters. Christian community is family by adoption, as God weaves divergent strands into a tapestry of divine providence. By God the Father's adoption, I became his child, and I left the home I made with Satan and his minions. Colossians 1:13 says, "For He rescued us from the domain of darkness, and transferred us to the kingdom of His beloved Son." I can rest into this verse and feel its contours. Adoption establishes my identity in Christ, my inheritance through Christ, and my mission because of Christ. Adoption is always both/and: it is about orphaned children and orphaned image bearers who lose the status of orphan through permanent sonship.

> Adoption is the only way to gospel identity.

Adoption is not a second-choice inclusion; it is the only way to gospel identity. An adopted person receives all rights, privileges, and family history. Likewise, our identity as Christians is not divided among factions. Strangers and enemies become brothers and sisters through Christ's blood. Hospitality in the home, neighborhood, and church starts with adoption and ends with keeping the Lord's Day together, because the purpose of our adoption is worship.

Hospitality in the Home Is Renewing

Kent and I adopted all four of our children, and not to compensate for my infertility. Likewise, God the Father's adoption of you and me was not done to compensate for something lacking. Adoption creates belonging that weaves lives together beyond gene pools and genetic codes. But it also creates an identity crisis. It is supposed to. Russell Moore puts it best: "None of us likes to think we were adopted. We assume we're natural-born children, with a right to all of this grace, to all of this glory."[1]

But we who are in Christ lay claim to an alien righteousness, and a new heritage through adoption. And out of our adoption, God springs a new sense of belonging and homestead. This newness of life should change the way our home looks and acts.

When we gather with people for a meal and family devotions

in our not-by-invitation-only home, we do this to be renewed by the Spirit of God. We are refreshed by each other's company, by the food that nourishes us, and by the Word of God, which we read and sing from the psalter. This is the regular pattern. No matter how bad your day was, this—and praying about your awful day, if you like—is what, by God's grace, we will do.

In our over-structured world, this might seem like a ridiculous luxury. Where are the soccer practices, the late nights at the office, and the reading clubs? Why aren't Kent and I too busy to do this? Because it matters a lot, that's why. Sometimes Kent, as a pastor, has a meeting with the elders at night, or a home visit or a counseling appointment. But for the most part, and because Kent and I value hospitality more than we do privacy or personal achievement, on Thursday night and on the Lord's Day, we are, by God's grace, here, ready to open the door to others.

Psalter—hymnal that puts the book of Psalms from the Bible to music.

This is not just a family tradition, something that we do to demonstrate a value and demarcate a family identity. God uses practices to unfold plans, callings, and missions. This fact— that practices unfold plans—became startlingly clear when my children and I recently read *The Hiding Place*, by Corrie ten Boom. The book begins with some simple practices that Casper ten Boom, the family patriarch, had in place. Every morning, after breakfast, he read from one chapter of the Old Testament. Every evening, after dinner, he read from one chapter of the New Testament. Because he was the neighborhood watchmaker, he often had clients and other people from the neighborhood at his table—believers and unbelievers, Gentiles and Jews, rich and poor. They ate, talked, listened to Scripture, and God used the time that they invested in this way to build community When unmitigated evil unleashed itself in Holland, they already had a community in place, carved out of neighbors, Scripture, and doing life together. They didn't know what for, but they were ready. First in their home and later in Hitler's concentration camps, Corrie and Betsie shared the gospel, their food, their lives, and their sufferings. They never had a plan, but they always had a practice. They had a practice of biblical communal living, and God used them to do great things for his kingdom and glory.

But what about us? What about our homes? What stands between us and doing life with others? What barriers or values have become idols that prevent us from establishing community from our homes? Here are ten points I recently came across on Pastor David Murray's excellent blog, headhearthand.org. Pastor David says that we are too busy, too selfish, too functional, too proud, too fearful, too safe, too superficial, too brainwashed, too competitive, and too un-Christlike. I agree.

So where do we begin? How do we create community together in this, our age of anxiety, phobia, fear, and stranger danger? How do we break bread together when there is a war against gluten raging everywhere we turn? How do we include people we do not yet know into our lives when we teach our children to beware of strangers? How do we break down the barriers between host and guest? Who are our neighbors, anyway? Would we know them without those handy window decals?

The barriers to seeing our homes as a Christian habitus—a lifegiving, Christ-honoring community—mount high. I hear excuses every day, usually coming out of my own mouth: I homeschool; I have small children whose ability to be influenced by sin rules my fretting heart; my neighbors are too busy and are never at home, anyway; I'm an introvert; I'm busy writing books and serving the church. My house is not neat enough, or decorated well enough to receive guests. (Really. I recently returned home from a two-day away speaking engagement trip to find our beloved cat stuck and struggling to release himself from the two-day old maple syrup cementing him on the kitchen table. Don't ask how this happened. Kent and the children have no idea who allowed this to happen.)

Maybe before we jump to *how* we need to start with *why*. Why create community from our homes? Who needs it? Why isn't our Facebook family enough, or our internet community? Why do we have to be close enough to touch each other, for real? And why does God call me to claim as my people those who are so different from me?

What does a Christian covenant home committed to hospitality provide to our world? How does it nurture people, support people in their needs, spread the gospel in deed and word, and provide the landscape for friendship of the kind that builds bridges?

1) A hospitality home creates places of compassion.

Compassion means "with suffering."

Compassion means "with suffering" and a hospitality home generates a way to practice accompanied suffering, standing with and for each other, and being there for each other without an appointment. (Scheduling a lunch date two weeks from Tuesday simply does not serve people who are dangerously and chronically lonely.)

2) A hospitality home creates opportunities to love the unlovely, because you, Christian, have much to learn from them, and you, perhaps, need them more than they need you.

3) A hospitality home provides a first-chair seat to abide in the family of God's orchestra.

4) A hospitality home invites the participants to put stock in the resonating effect of small things, little gestures, tiny connections, and puny attempts at connection.

5) A hospitality home creates a boundary set by God to help you not sin against him.

Where to Start in Making Your Home a Hospitality Home?

Hospitality begins with loving the stranger. So the first reality check to do is this: if everybody at your table is on the same page and from the same side of the tracks, you aren't practicing hospitality. You may need to do a heart-check here as well. It is easier to feel safe in the company of people who are just like you, who struggle and identify with the same things you do. But creating a safe space is not the ultimate point or purpose of Christian hospitality.

The word *hospitality* transliterates from the Greek word *philoxenia*, or love of the stranger. But hospitality is not a New

Testament phenomenon. We first see hospitality at work in the Old Testament, when Lot rushes to meet the strangers at the gate in Sodom to spare them from harm. Lot felt a moral responsibility to shelter them. He recognized something in the stranger that was a mirror reflection of him. We need to stop here. Do we recognize strangers as our kin? He recognized them and he acted on his recognition in a direct and forthright way. Do we? Do we recognize ourselves as having been strangers once?

Philoxenia — love of the stranger.

1) *Community begins when we remember that we were all once strangers to God.* We all started out as strangers and enemies, to God and to each other. We see this in Jesus' words in the gospel of Matthew: "For I was hungry, and you gave Me something to eat; I was thirsty and you gave Me something to drink; I was a stranger and you invited Me in; naked, and you clothed me; I was sick, and you visited Me; I was in prison and you came to Me" (Matt. 25:35–36). When we feel entitled to God's grace, we can never get at the core sentiment behind these words. What would it take to see Jesus in the homeless and the homely?

American poet William Stafford (1914–1993) in his poem "Easter Morning" defines an encounter with Jesus like this: "You just shiver alive and are left standing/there suddenly brought to account: saved." Stafford then portrays the challenge of discerning Jesus in the stranger, because sometimes you open your door or open your heart and you get Satan instead. He writes: "the slick voice can sell you anything even/Hell, which is what you're getting by listening."

The risk is laid bare in Jesus' words: when we fail to see him in others, we cheapen the power of the image of God to shine over the darkness of the world. When we always see him in others, we fail to discern that we live in a fallen world, where Satan knows our address.

As we pray for the Holy Spirit to give us discernment about and love for others, we do well to remember that justification is "an act of God's free grace, wherein he pardons all our sins, and accepts us as righteous in his sight, only for the righteousness of Christ imputed to us, and received by faith alone."[2] We do well to remember that we do not justify ourselves, and to heed this warning, in the words of the German martyr Dietrich Bonhoeffer, "self-justification and judging others go together, as justification by grace and serving others go together."[3]

2) *Community begins when we defy Stranger Danger—even when some strangers are dangerous.* Kent and I do a lot of local public speaking these days on hospitality and loving the stranger. We like to minister together, and we balance each other well, I think. One routine day in May 2014, Kent and I gathered up the kids and headed to a local Baptist church to give a talk about loving the stranger. Before we left the house, we gave the dogs their treats: Kongs with frozen peanut butter. (I keep a supply in the freezer.) We were in a hurry, and we left our Bibles on the table. They were opened to the gospel of Luke. Before I left my house for the last time, I looked back. I saw that the Bibles made a rough square on the dining room table, with some LEGOs and dinosaurs as well and one lightsaber. We locked the doors behind us, both the knob and the deadbolt.

Our talk went well, we think. We hope we encouraged other Christian families to open their homes and see Jesus in those in need. After the Q&A, we piled the kids back in the car and took the familiar drive back home. It was a good day, and I was looking forward to getting home, making coffee, finishing the laundry, icing my injured foot, and reading the last chapter of *Prince Caspian* to the kids.

I knew something was wrong as soon as I keyed in. My ever-hyper, effervescent, and effusive golden retriever, Sally, was cowering in the corner, hurt and scared. Clothes and dining room plates and family pictures were strewn everywhere. As we walked into the kitchen, we saw it. A window had been snapped at the frame and popped out with a crowbar. The robbers had to stand on the large dog feeding station to crawl in the broken window, so obviously they weren't threatened by big dogs. Covering our open Bibles were those things the robbers discarded—some of my mom's china, and the golden-colored bowl that Kent uses for baptisms. Seeing the golden baptism bowl next to the Bibles was the only sensible thing in this whole picture.

I looked at my hurt dog and kissed her face. She wagged at me, but her heart wasn't in it. I walked through the house as if underwater. Sally trailed cautiously behind. The robbers yanked the TV off the wall, leaving holes in the wall and floor, where I suspect they must have dropped it. The drawers to all dressers hung open and their contents were strewn everywhere: socks, geography puzzles, math videos, marbles, the dog's heart pills. The robbers stole all of my jewelry, including my engagement ring, an heirloom that had been in Kent's family for five generations. I always feared I would hurt or lose it if I wore it, especially during summer months, when my hands are deep in garden dirt when they are not holding children or turning book pages or kneading communion bread. I had stared at it just that morning, contemplating whether it was safe to wear today, and turned down my last chance.

My mother, who recently moved to a retirement home, gifted me with her family jewelry, for safe keeping and memory's sake. They took it all. But the close-range grief was Sally, my golden. Bruised. Sad. Shivering. When the police came, they explained it like this: big dogs are in the way, and robbers either shoot them or bludgeon them. They took our information, fingerprinted every doorknob and door frame, and left more mess and dirt in their wake.

It was awful to be robbed.

It was ironic to realize that as we advocated for hospitality to the stranger, he beat my dog and walked off with the goods, vandalizing the house just for good measure.

We all were in a state of shock. My children's anxiety rocketed through the roof. Not one of us found *OK* for months.

But when it was dinnertime, our people surrounded us. I was not serving, but receiving. Our people set the table. Matthew, an exchange student from Singapore, was moving in to our house that night as the residence hall at the University of North

Carolina was closing. It was so good to have his calming spirit home to help. Susanna was just leaving Duke, where she works, and picked up a rotisserie chicken and butter pecan ice cream on her way to our house. Just because she knew I would need butter pecan.

As is my routine, when I moved the prized Kroger chicken from its plastic bed to the pan, Sally got the plastic container covered in chicken grease and juice. She settled down with it in her favorite posture, nose in the corner and back feet splayed like a water buffalo in yoga (as if she could hide ninety pounds simply by giving us her backside). She held the plastic dish between her paws, and started to perk up when more people came over. Our homeschool dad friends came with tools and Scripture, dropping their lawn care and important executive jobs to help. And after dinner and prayer and Bible reading and a psalm, we started with a bucket and a rag, garbage bags and the vacuum cleaner.

It was hard to be robbed.

It was hard to have God test so powerfully and privately what we proclaimed publicly—that even if you are hurt, people can't take the things that matter most and that will survive to the new heavens and earth: your soul and his Word.

The day after we were robbed, Kent pushed the grill to the front yard, where the picnic table was already waiting. Then, he posted three things on the neighborhood email list: we were robbed; robbers took stuff, but not things of eternal value—the Word of God and the life souls of people—and we would love for everyone to join us for burgers and hot dogs on the Lord's Day, starting at three o'clock. As Susanna pointed out, that Lord's Day was Mother's Day, and my husband had just invited 300 people to our front yard. Well, that is how things go at the Butterfields'! It was a joy-filled time, with hot dogs and kids and water guns and meeting new and old friends. Twenty-one neighbors showed up, and most of our church family as well. And when our unbelieving neighbors asked how we were holding up, Kent was able to share the gospel with new legitimacy, because where God is in your loss matters more to a skeptical, unbelieving, and watching world than where God is in your plenty.

It feels awful to come home and find your house ransacked, holes in the walls, your underwear touched by the wrong hands, your journals and vitamins tossed all over the floor, and the dog you raised from mitten-size bruised and fearful. It was humiliating to not be sovereign over locked doors and engagement rings. It was painful to realize that he who is sovereign allowed this to happen, for his glory and for my own good (Rom. 8:28).

But it must feel deceptive and sinister to be the people who robbed me, bad in the way that a coat of paint and comfort of neighbors with rotisserie chicken and butter pecan ice cream can't fix. It must create a hole in your humanity that you know will swallow up everyone you love. I realized that night that it was more awful to be my robber than me. It must be a spine-chilling nightmare from which you never awake to realize in the flesh the evil that you know you are capable of, and to get away with it.

3) *Community begins when we remember that perfect love casts out fear (1 John 4:18).*

We sometimes fear that our neighbors will bring problems and issues into our homes that we are not ready to discuss in front of our children. We pit the command to nurture and teach our children in the fear and admonition of the Lord against the command to love our neighbor.

We need to stop and think about this. On the one hand, we of course must protect our children from harm. And, on the other hand, we must not presume that sheltering them will accomplish this. Perhaps our children need to know that when they confront doubts and fears, sexual temptations, and moral and faith crises, that we will not be shocked, offended, or hurt by this reality.

Our children need to know that we know how serious the enemy is, how "alien" and yet powerful our righteousness in Christ is, and how deep and wide and big and powerful our sin can become if we hide it.

But if we have had a ministry to the lost, and if our children have seen us embracing our neighbors who are struggling, or burdened, or falling under the weight of sin and tragedy, perhaps, just perhaps, our children will trust us with their deep things. Perhaps they will remember that we embraced our neighbors and strangers, that we loved them and prayed for them, and that we were not jostled or unsettled to share block parties or BBQs, our churches and our homes, with troubled people. Perhaps our love of those image bearers, all of them, especially the difficult ones, will be a pledge to our children that the mosaics of their private lives are safe with us.

4) *Community begins when we remember that God uses us as living epistles*, and the openness or inaccessibility of our homes and hearts stands between life and death, victory or defeat, grace or shame for most people.

Consider with me the tension of 1 Corinthians 10:13: "No temptation has overtaken you but such that is common to man; and God is faithful, who will not allow you to be tempted beyond what you are able, but with the temptation will provide the way of escape also, so that you will be able to endure it." This passage speaks to the intensity, the loneliness, the danger of temptation. It also speaks to the lived tension of applying faith to our trials, and then waiting, waiting, waiting for that way of escape to present itself where it was not before. Have you ever thought that you, your house, and your time were not your own, but rather, God's ordained way of escape for someone?

I think about this every Lord's Day morning as I am preparing food for the day, praying about who will join us. Behind the peaceful surface, it is a day of warfare. Perhaps you had not realized this, but the Lord's Day is a terrible day of temptation and sin for many people. Without the moorings of a vital church community and Christian church family and the fourth commandment ("keep the Lord's Day holy")—and indeed, sometimes with them— it is a day awash in the twin churnings of the world: personal achievement and material acquisition. But the fourth commandment begins with the verb "remember"— one of the most pressing and recurring commands in Scripture. It says, "Remember the Sabbath day, to keep it holy" (Ex. 20:8).

Memory is best when it is collective. You see, your job is not just to keep the Sabbath holy for you, but to live in such a way that you enable a co-operative kinship, a fellowship of believers, a place at the table, available to others and not by invitation only.

We keep the Sabbath in global and communal ways by sharing ordinary means of grace given to us by God. But the Lord's Day is not "family day." It is not "just us" day. If you preserve this day for isolation or separation, you may unwittingly be causing your sister to stumble into sin.

In *Life Together,* Bonhoeffer comments,

> Sin demands to have a man by himself. It withdraws him from the community. The more isolated a person is, the more extractive will be the power of sin over him, and the more deeply he becomes involved in it, the more disastrous is his isolation.[4]

My favorite day of the week is the Lord's Day, and I want to share that with others. Kent and I open our home after worship and mercy ministry[5] to anyone who can come. We must. We remember what it was like to not have a place to go after worship, the odd tearing away of the body as each goes off to his own corner of the world while the benediction still rings in your ears. It is cruel to the people in the church to have no place to go on the Lord's Day, no place to belong and no place to be needed. We must work hard to search out people who are easy to neglect or overlook. We need each other.

When we are too functional, we forget the point of hospitality in the home: fellowship, not entertainment. Don't let pride stop you from opening your home. Ignore the cat hair on the couch (or in the mac and cheese). It likely won't kill anyone as decisively as loneliness will. Add as much water to the pot to stretch the soup. If you run out of food, make pancakes, and put the kids in charge of making that meal. See how much fun that is!

And know that someone is spared from another humiliating fall into internet pornography because he is instead walking with you and your kids and dogs, as you share the Lord's Day, one model of how the Lord gives you daily grace and a way of escape. Know that someone is spared the fear and darkness of depression because she is needed at your house, always on the Lord's Day, the day she is never alone, but instead safely in community, where her place at the table is needed and necessary and relied upon.

Know that someone is drawn into Christ's love because the Bible reading and psalm singing that come at the close of the meal include everyone, and that it reminds us that no one is scapegoated in this Christ-bearing community. Know that host and guest are equally precious and fragile, and that you will play both roles throughout the course of this life. The doors here open wide. They must.

5) *Community begins with an intentional plan to open the doors of the covenant community* and then toss over your shoulders and carry home someone who cannot walk there herself.

Have you ever considered becoming a licensed foster parent? When you become a licensed foster parent, you have access to children in need and families in need. Even if the needs a child presents exceed your capacity and you therefore have to say no to a home placement, you are deep in the prayer loop. You can take that child to the throne of grace even if you cannot take her home. When you work with the foster care system, you meet a large population who needs the Lord and the Lord's people. And adding to your family by adoption is a daily mirror of God's saving work. I love being part of a transracial family, as it also reflects the diversity of the kingdom that we will one day inherit. God wants the church to be the frontline of hope and family for orphans. Don't be afraid to show up. God will meet you there.

If many families in the church go through foster parent training together, you can become your own prayer and support group. You can provide the extra help that single covenant Christians who are members of your church may need to also become foster parents. There are too many teenagers in foster care, waiting for homes, waiting for adoption, or waiting for the mentors they need to help them in all transitions into

161

adulthood, and most of these teenagers will only be placed in single households. Single Christians may be uniquely called for this pivotal crisis of life for teenagers in foster care.

Even if adopting or foster parenting is not your calling, you may find yourself training to be a guardian *ad litem* or a Big Brother or Big Sister. Perhaps you can partner with another family in the church to keep sibling groups together, or use your training to provide respite care to a family in the church with special needs foster children. You can be Aaron holding up Moses' arms when you lock arms with someone in the adoption and foster care world.

6) *Community begins when your home becomes a safe place to grieve.* Do you know someone who has buried a child or a spouse? Someone who has miscarried? Someone whose same-sex desires nag at her day after day, causing her to wonder if God has forgotten her? Do you know someone whose singleness makes him feel rejected, or whose infertility makes her feel like God's promises are not real and not really for her? Do you know someone who wears loneliness as sackcloth? The home is the place to move in close—and stay there. Home is where isolation is broken. Home is where suffering meets accompaniment. Home is the best place to incorporate people who need you into the rhythms of life together. Perhaps God gave you a home for just such a purpose. Set aside a weekly and consistent time and place, and pray that the Lord will fill that. Be intentional. Are you good company for the suffering? Why not?

7) *Community begins when we learn that hospitality is for the good of the giver.* We have so many barriers to practicing community in the one place that it is vitally and daily needed: the Christian home. But we fear that we will not measure up, that we are failing to protect our children in this dangerous world, that we will get in over our heads with people and their needs and that they will suck us dry in the process. We know that God commands us to practice hospitality for his glory and for

the protection of the unloved, but in what way is the creation of Christian community intended for the good of the giver?

Doing life together helps us to realize that people and theological or political positions are different. People are always more complex than the ideas that they embrace.

Hospitality helps us to keep a guard over our mouth.

Practicing hospitality helps us to keep a guard over our mouth (Psalm 141) while rendering Ephesians 4:29 a verse of immediate urgency: "Let no unwholesome word proceed from your mouth, but only such a word as is good for edification according to the need of the moment, so that it will give grace to those who hear." We live with a draught of bloody, faithful grace, given freely but agonizingly by Christ and bestowed to us, for our union with Christ, our sanctification through Christ, and communion of the saints.

As people gather around your table, Christ heals the parched land of their hearts as you share words of salt and light, informally, as it spills into the needs of the moment, with humility, patience, gentleness, with Bibles and psalters open. Doing life together means silence or sadness turns into prayer without "calling for prayer requests" or happening to have your crisis fall within the Wednesday night prayer meeting time frame. It happens when Bibles or psalters flip open as tension or division escalates, not to avoid the conflict, but to ask Jesus to enter it.

Because it is not "just us" here, because you have chosen company with hurting people, you are not going to let your guard down. This, by God's grace, will not be a day that turns into a night of torment, as you replay what you said and wish that you could erase it. Your children are learning how to share the gospel with fluency, and how to love it before a watching world. And you see gospel fruit in your role in God's community as a helper and healer, as a server and a caregiver, and as receiver and needer. You have sharpened your prayers with heartache over people you would never know without this ministry. You count it joy—even when you are dead tired and somebody put a hole in your wall—knowing that God will magnify your efforts. You partner with others to make your homes places where Jesus could rest his head.

Hospitality in the Neighborhood

G. K. Chesterton once quipped, "We make our friends; we make our enemies, but God makes our next door neighbor.... We have to love our neighbor because he is there." The nearness of our neighbor is providential, as God never gets the address wrong.

Last year, Kent preached a series of sermons on hospitality, a rare foray into topical preaching. It was that important, he said, that he got out of his comfort zone of expository explication through a whole Bible book and took the risk of shaking up the church.

After he preached this sermon series, he and I read the book, *The Art of Neighboring*, by Jay Pathak and Dave Runyon.[6] I liked it so much that I bought a few copies and gave them to Christian neighbors we hoped would partner with us in fulfilling what is on the surface a simple command: love your neighbor.

Summers in North Carolina are memorable for June bugs, humidity, and long night walks, when many neighbors are also out walking. That first summer in Durham, Kent and I would look longingly at our front yard, wanting to fill it with neighbors. We were hungry to get to know people better and get serious about serving our neighbors. That's when Kent decided to apply one simple thing that we learned from *The Art of Neighboring*: put lawn chairs and tables in the front yard. So, he and our neighbor Ryan built a picnic table, and then positioned it in the front yard under our massive oak tree where everyone could see it. The kids and I painted it neon green (so that you could really see it). Soon, neighbors started gathering there. It became a nice spot to stop and talk, re-apply bug spray, grab water, and talk. Eventually, our pastor friend Micah Ramsey hung a tire swing off of the sturdy oak. It is now a perfect gathering spot. Not by invitation only. Come as you are.

After the picnic table assumed its front yard spot, we wrote this email and distributed it to everyone we knew in the neighborhood. Here is what it said:

> Dear Friends,
> Please join with us at the green picnic table on the front lawn of the Butterfields' on Thursday, August 15, 2013, at 7 p.m. for our inaugural and weekly prayer walk. We will pray with our eyes and our hearts open, seeking to bring glory to our Triune God and raise our neighborhood needs to the Throne of Grace. Those walking without kids, dogs, and strollers might also bring a pencil and paper to collect prayer and mercy requests and gather information about our neighbors' needs. We will meet back at the picnic table at eight o'clock and close our evening with singing a psalm and creating an action plan to meet mercy needs. Please forward this email to anyone in the neighborhood who might like to join us.
> Love in Christ,
> Rosaria (for the Butterfields)

Thursday night arrived. Neighbors drew near from all directions. Some came because of the email. Others tied in because they wondered what kind of a party we were having. Kent gathered us together and we prayed for God to hear us.

Something transformative happens when we pray with our neighbors like this, something we commit to doing each Thursday night. Something that has become, for us, the touchstone of our neighboring. Every Thursday night we host a neighborhood open house, and we launch it by taking back the streets in prayer.

When things become a tradition, they acquire a comfort and a predictability about them. But prayer is never predictable. If Jesus enters, even that which is rehearsed is never routine. Today, it is established that on Thursday night we will pray with our neighbors and gather together for fellowship. Thursday night neighborhood ministry is now like a tried and true friend. But our first night of prayer and fellowship happened as if in a dream.

This is how I remember that first Thursday night prayer walk.

We meet at the picnic table and introduce ourselves. There are many people here whose face I recognize but whose name I do not know. We break naturally into groups of two and three, unintentionally gender-segregating when the kids on wheels want to race down a big hill and the moms with strollers weren't hankering for broken bones. The men take the cross-country route, with the big kids, and the women, dogs, toddlers, and strollers stay on the path. We pray aloud in unhurried, unrehearsed, unrestrained, and unworried tones. We stir prayers and interruptions like they all go together in the same pot of soup. We stop to talk to neighbors and ask them to tell us who they are and what they need. Life layers prayer. No such thing as an interruption. Children need sippy cups, dogs need cleaning up after, and prayer marches on. Sometimes neighbors join us for a block, just to hear what we are praying for.

And then it hits me: this prayer walk is itself a breed and species of Christian hospitality.

Extending arms wide, we draw others into our posture of ambulatory bended knee, eyes wide open. We go to God together for mercy, grace, increase. Hospitality starts with emptiness, and waits together for God to complete us. On a prayer walk, we seek to give that which we do not yet have, but by faith behold as inevitable: God's promise to keep his covenant, and the reality that he has already set apart great blessings he will only grant through prayer.

But a righteous and holy God only hears the prayers of his redeemed people, of those who, by grace, come to his throne in the alien robes of Christ's righteousness and blood. We all come with blood on our hands, but whose blood is it? And this prayer walk is risky business. "Even though you multiply prayers, I will not listen. Your hands are covered in blood," so declares God in Isaiah 1:15. That we cannot come to a holy God with our virtuous intentions and high-minded deeds simply does not fly with my unsaved neighbors. The exclusivity of Christ tramples on our American confidence and self-absorption. That raises the bar of responsibility on this prayer walk. Indeed, how will our unsaved neighbors come to the banquets of prayer without the intercession of God's people? In the Acts 17 world in which we live, how will our unsaved neighbors know that the deepest meaning of their pain is that their prayers do not (yet) resonate with God?

When you stand with the suffering, you draw no lines.

When should we share and model the good news that only rings authentic because of the bad news that precedes us all? What if we are called to grieve with those who suffer because of sin and disobedience? When you stand with the suffering, you draw no lines. Neighbors stand close enough to touch.

This is messy business, this prayer walk. We don't bother with formalities like whose turn it is to pray. We jump in. The Holy Spirit does not play card dealer.

Sometimes we pause in front of a house that we know is struggling with something, so we pray like this:

> Lord, remember your covenant with your people. In Christ, there is meaning, and purpose and suffering in our pain. Please bring the Jones family to salvation, we pray, so that Bill and Jean can know your comfort in such a time as this. May this give you praise and glory. Thank you that we can pray, that we can walk, and that we can hear the laughter of our children as we do this. Thank you that we can pray with eyes open. Help us to move in close to our neighbors in their pain. Cause us to be good company for the suffering. Forgive us for the distance that we keep from others.

Sometimes our ignorance rebukes us. Why don't we know the names of the people who live in the house on the corner, the one with the screen door that is perpetually torn? Why do we know our neighbors best by polite and anonymous waves? We pray that as God may allow us to know real stories of real people, that we would cherish this information as jewels and never gossip

167

or betray them. We pray that God would forgive our sin of not noticing, not caring, and not initiating friendships. We repent. We do not love our neighbors like ourselves. As we walk and pray and stop and talk, we learn about the people who share our blocks. We pray for them by name, asking God to help us put away distractions and put on love.

Why do this? Why not just have the Christian neighbors over for a BBQ, or football, or board games? Why not just invite the people we know are Christians to join us in our living rooms and pray with the doors closed? Why not exclusively surround ourselves with people who are just like us?

We commit ourselves to praying with and for our neighbors every Thursday night in order to remember. We remember what it was like before the Holy Spirit chiseled our stony heart soft. We remember what it was like before the blood of Jesus pumped our hearts whole. We remember the night terrors and the midmorning anxiety attacks, the unraveled good intentions of daily inventing ourselves and snowballing rules through which we hoped we could function. We remember what it was like to crack under the weight of this, and the loneliness of having no place to go but drugs, alcohol, sex, or lies. We remember our own predatory sin, and its legacy, and how for nothing that we could do or offer, God reached down and brought us to himself. We remember the throne of grace rising from the rubble, we remember that repentance is the threshold to God, and we want to invite others to come.

Before we started prayer walking we heard rumor of need.

One of our neighbors has Lou Gehrig's disease. He is forty and his youngest child is two. Another neighbor has an abdominal tumor the size of a twenty-four-week-old fetus. Many neighbors have lost jobs, and the stress in their households rises high. Some neighbors are wearing telltale scarves and losing hair, but we don't know their names. We don't want to bring up the "C" word without at least having a first name to go with it. Some neighbors have households hard to discern. Divorced? Widowed? Shut in? Who knows? Who could know when we are too busy to care? There is a cul-de-sac at the end of the block called "Widow's Corner," because almost every household in that circle is inhabited by a widow. But I don't know the first name of even one of those souls, even though I walk my dogs through this circle every day. Because they are all "shut ins," I couldn't recognize one of these women's faces if my life depended on it.

How did we get to this place where we are so estranged? Once we hear their story, will we follow through on what we know? Or will we duck and run? How do we gather our arms wide and hold fast? We need each other in this prayer walk, this Christian walk. All by ourselves, we will forget, lose heart, and start walking the dogs with our smartphones glued to our ears or thumbs.

After one mile of prayer, the creeping fall darkness corners us. When we return to the picnic table, the children start running barefoot in the grass while the men finish up a list of mercy needs. I go to the kitchen to assemble something to eat for our guests, and while I am walking in the dark, I am marveling over how many neighbors came to pray. Was it fifteen? Twenty-five when you count the kids? I ponder over what I have in the kitchen for all of these people. I flick on the switch and the harsh light blinds me for a minute. I shut it off and work in the dark. I bring out a half watermelon, a loaf of fresh bread, and some honey. I move as if in a dream or underwater. My neighbors are still here, captivated by a mile high of prayer.

Something has changed among us. Some barrier of intimacy has been shattered. How? In the heavens? On the streets? Both? I slice the watermelon and dollop big spoonfuls of honey on homemade bread. The children finally sprawl, munch, lick sticky fingers, and fold into laps and on hips and on the grass. The lush full moon suspends low tonight, as it does in North Carolina in August. It almost looks like the trees can brush against it. The stars come out, and so do the psalters. I recall Psalm 147:3–4: "He heals the brokenhearted and binds up their wounds. He counts the number of stars; He gives names to all of them."

Does the God who numbers and names the stars do the same with the broken hearts and promises of our neighbors? Is this prayer walking one way of gathering the fragments of pain, and giving all of the pieces to the God who made me and takes care of me?

As the children droop limp on shoulders, Kent passes out the psalters. We gravitate to the street light, so that we can see. Only Kent and I have sung together before. We begin to sing from the 23rd Psalm.[7]

> *The Lord's my Shepherd, I'll not want,*
> *He makes me down to lie*
> *In pastures green; He leadeth me*
> *The quiet waters by.*
>
> *My soul He doth restore again;*
> *And me to walk doth make*
> *Within the paths of righteousness,*
> *E'en for His own name's sake.*
> (Psalm 23B, stanzas 1–2)

Singing *a cappella* on a hot summer night without preparation forges our intimacy and vulnerability. As we breathe together, I thank the God who gave us this breath. And as we break into parts, my heart sparkles with the sudden surprise that Donna's rich alto voice vibrates in perfect partnership with Kristin's soprano. I leap into the soprano descant, and we all breathe together. I'm getting goosebumps. We all could have been neighbors for fifty years and not have known this. Secrets and mysteries are unveiling all around us.

> *Yea, though I walk in death's dark vale,*
> *Yet will I fear no ill;*
> *For Thou art with me, and Thy rod*
> *And staff me comfort still.*
>
> *A table Thou hast furnished me*
> *In presence of my foes;*
> *My head Thou dost with oil annoint,*
> *And my cup overflows.* (stanzas 3–4)

As we sing together, I realize something: we pray with strangers in the hopes that they will not remain strangers, but rather be transformed into sisters and brothers with whom we will sing in full voice into eternity. Hospitality gives God glory by revealing him as the provider and the host. It does not steal glory from God by giving the appearance of self-sufficiency. God is the author of the banquet. We are—at best—one of the means. Who knew God had so much mercy and intimacy in store for us this night?

Goodness and mercy all my life
Shall surely follow me;
And in God's house forevermore
My dwelling place shall be. (stanza 5)

Joggers stop to listen.

The predictable parade of rolling garbage cans pause en route to the weekly resting place at the curb. Ears bend. I look up at the stars, and I know I am small, a broken reed, a bent arrow. And yet, God chooses to use even the likes of me.

Our psalm ends, and only now do we hear the chorus of tree frogs and crickets.

I have never before experienced community prayer as an act of hospitality before this night. I finally get it. God has blessings designed for us, measured out, prearranged, that he will only dispense by prayer. Why? Because prayer changes us to receive what it shakes the gates of heaven to give. I shudder to think of the lost blessings, buried under the rubble of busy schedules and fear.

It is different now, two years later. Thursdays are still neighbor nights. During the spring and summer months, we walk and pray until 8 p.m., meeting at the now-fading green picnic table under the shady oak tree in our front yard. Sometimes it is hard to get going. What will I say? What if I just repeat the same thing, over and over again?

One Thursday last September, I was feeling especially skittish about praying. Many of my usual praying neighbors were sick at home, and I was tired and getting ready for a trip the next day. It was much more practical for me to do laundry and pack than head out the door to pray. When I walked to the green picnic table, I had no idea who would meet me there. My dear friend Kristin met me with the stroller, and we started off. The bigger kids ran ahead, and it was a sweet night, just me and Kristin, her toddler in the stroller, my dog on a leash. The husbands prayed and kept pace with the big kids.

Kristin and I did not walk and pray more than one block when the Lord sent a meteor of hope and purpose. As we approached different houses, neighbors started to come out of their front doors to stop us and ask us to pray about a family member's cancer, or the impending death of a favorite aunt. Not just one neighbor, but neighbors. Block after block. We gathered some in close and prayed together holding shoulders that were shaking in grief. It has never taken us that long to complete the "prayer loop." But the Lord sent so many hurting hearts who needed a hand on a shoulder and a heart for Jesus.

We returned home late. The older children had already started to watch *The Pink Panther* on the computer and our husbands were talking in the kitchen and we could both feel it, that powerful reality that had we not shown up to pray, immeasurable blessings would have slipped through our fingers unnoticed. And perhaps even slipped through the heavens. That night we learned the art of showing up.

In the late fall and winter, we gather in different neighbors' kitchens or living rooms. If the weather is good, we settle on the porch. If we meet at Ray's house, he makes a strong pot of decaffeinated coffee. If we meet at Donna and Bob's, the little kids settle in the most comfortable TV room you could imagine, wrap themselves in handmade quilts, and watch *Charlie Brown* while the adults pray. After years of this, we have noticed that our doors are more open, the rhythms of our days more transparent. This makes a good bridge to the asking of hard questions and the offer of a steady hand. Weekly, and by God's grace, our lives and needs as neighbors unfold together and before the throne of grace.

Hospitality within the Covenant of Church Membership: Belonging to One Another

The church is Christ's bride. It is a visible sign that you are a member of the family of God. Just like you belong to a specific and visible human family, if you are a covenant member of a church, you belong in a specific way to one, singular, local congregation. Covenant membership in the visible church should mean something and translate something to a watching world. Your neighbors know details about you even if they don't (yet) know your name. Mine know that I have an electric fence for my dogs, and that I turn on the porch light at 5 a.m. I believe church membership could be something that also translates across the picket fence. What if being a member of a Christ-honoring church communicated the attributes of God to the watching world? What if it revealed that we are a people safe with your secrets, able to help with your needs, willing to stand by you in times of grief, and able to put the hand of the suffering into the hand of the Savior? What if membership meant belonging to one another in a deep and abiding way?

As Christians we are members of both the visible and the invisible church. The visible church refers to a local body, made up of believers and unbelievers.

There is a special friendship, a deep and abiding covenant, that could bleed through one believer to another who are both bound to Christ through church membership. Membership could be strong enough to uphold those who are weak, fallen, broken, repenting, and struggling sheep. Church membership could create greater intimacy with others who have taken covenant vows.

But does it?

Imagine how different our world would be if this was so.

Church exists as Christ's bride, and as such, its purpose is to give glory to God and stand as a testimony to the truth of Scripture from age to age. Members of a church take vows and make a covenant with God and with each other. In my denomination, the Reformed Presbyterian Church, when a person seeks covenant of church membership, after meeting with the elders and taking a class on the covenant of church membership, she stands before the body and gives assent to these official vows:

> 1) Do you believe the Scriptures of the Old and New Testaments to be the Word of God, the only infallible rule of faith and life?
> 2) Do you believe in the one living and true God—Father, Son, and Holy Spirit, as revealed in the Scriptures?
> 3) Do you repent of your sin; confess your guilt and helplessness as a sinner against God; profess Jesus Christ, Son of God, as your Savior and Lord; and dedicate yourself to His service: Do you promise that you will endeavor to forsake all sin, and to conform your life to His teaching and example?
> 4) Do you promise to submit in the Lord to the teaching and government of this church as being based upon the Scriptures and described in substance in the *Constitution of the Reformed Presbyterian Church of North America*? Do you recognize your responsibility to work with others in the church and do you promise to support and encourage them in their service to the Lord? In case you should need correction in doctrine or life, do you promise to respect the authority and discipline of the church?
> 5) To the end that you may grow in the Christian life, do you promise that you will diligently read the Bible, engage in private prayer, keep the Lord's Day, regularly attend the worship services, observe the appointed sacraments, and give to the Lord's work as He shall prosper you?
> 6) Do you purpose to seek first the kingdom of God and His righteousness in all the relationships of life, faithfully to perform your whole duty as a true servant of Jesus Christ, and seek to win others to Him?
> 7) Do you make this profession of faith and purpose in the presence of God, in humble reliance upon His grace, as you desire to give your account with joy at the Last Great Day?

In *Secret Thoughts*, I shared with you that taking these vows explicitly marked me as a traitor in my LGBT community. To this day, when I hear my husband read these vows to new members, I experience a dulling dizziness, complex heartache about how much I have made my Lord endure, and awe at God's covenant love. That I now stand in Christ and with fellow believers daily reveals Christ's power to save.

In my denomination, all who make a profession of faith and publicly commit their lives to Christ take these vows. These vows are a matter of life and death. These vows—and the other doctrinal and confessional standards of my church—are important to examine. You should not take church membership lightly. These vows are a visible sign of union with Christ and communion with the saints. Membership is soul business, with a daily dose of earthly good.

The *Westminster Confession of Faith* (*WCF*) represents the church as both invisible and visible. Of the invisible church, it says this:

> The catholic or universal Church, which is invisible, consists of the whole number of the elect, that have been, are, or shall be gathered into one, under Christ the Head thereof; and is the spouse, the body, the fulness of Him that filleth all.[8]

The invisible church is that which God himself knows and ordains and contains. It is called "invisible" because it is invisible to us. It does not have a witness to a watching world. It is made up of all believers, across history, nation, and time. But it is, as its name suggests, invisible.

Because God cares to make himself known, he commands believers to be members of a visible church. Of the visible church, the *WCF* says:

> The visible Church, which is also catholic or universal under the Gospel…consists of all those throughout the world that profess the true religion; and of their children: and is the kingdom of the Lord Jesus Christ, the house and family of God, out of which there is no ordinary possibility of salvation.[9]

I am daily stunned by this: God made the church to stand as a visible witness to a watching world and to remain as a beacon. The visible church, made up of average people with plenty of problems, sin patterns, character flaws, annoying habits, and peculiar interests. The church remains as a beacon of who God is. Not the Christian family. Not the Christian college. Not individual celebrity Christians who do a lot and get a lot of attention for doing a lot. The church alone is commended by God to hold this privilege.

But two things distort the clear visibility of the true church: 1) the ways that sin disfigures each member of the church, and, 2) the reality of wolves in sheep's clothing who also take these vows. This is true across the wide range of denominations. There is no such thing as a pure denomination or church body. As G. I. Williamson says,

> Because there is evil in true believers while they are on earth, and because there is the appearance of faith and righteousness in hypocrites, the visible manifestation of the Church is never perfect.... Every attempt to realize the perfect Church (i.e., in which there are no hypocrites at all) is doomed to failure because the Church is invisible to us in exactly the sense that it would have to be visible to us to realize this goal.[10]

It baffles me that God permits the visible church to contain hypocrites, but my perplexity is not the yardstick of God's truth. Williamson explains it like this: "The true Church becomes visible, not by an identification of persons, but by an identification of presence."[11] It is not the presence of sin that renders a church worthy of the dust on your boots. Paul did not tell members of the church of Corinth to go find another church. Why?

Because the visible church is "the house and family of God." In the church, we are "members of the household of God" (Eph. 2:19, ESV), and as such, we belong one to another—"to those who belong to the family of believers" (Gal. 6:10). The church is a covenant community, where privileges and responsibilities belong to believers, their children, and their households (Gen. 17:9–14).

One of my favorite passages of Scripture, one that I roll over in my mind, my heart, my imagination, and my daily prayers, reminds us how the family of God exists to give its members comfort in times of affliction, loneliness, loss and despair.

In Mark 10, Jesus comforts Peter (and me) with these words:

29 Truly I say to you, there is no one who has left house or brothers or sisters or mother or father or children or farms, for My sake and for the gospel's sake,
30 but that he will receive a hundred times as much now in the present age, houses and brothers and sisters and mothers and children and farms, along with persecutions; and in the age to come, eternal life.

Through the people of God identified by membership in the visible church, the Lord gives us family. And this family makes up for our real loss and persecutions "a hundred times as much." The family of God is meant to reveal this to a skeptical, love-starved watching world.

The visible church is charged with gathering believers and growing them in the means of grace (Bible reading, private devotions, daily confession, fellowship), rightly administering the preached Word and the sacraments, and providing both teaching and ruling elders who discipline themselves and provide church members with pastoral oversight and counseling as we grow in sanctification and godliness, manifesting integrity, hospitality, and charity one to another. Martyn Lloyd-Jones deemed church membership as "the biggest honor which can come a man's way in this world."[12] I agree.

This is all very fine and good. Very lofty and noble and high-minded. But if each believer in my congregation took each vow to heart, we could be a transformed community, enfolding each other into vital fellowship and meaningful relationships. Membership is soul business, but its effect, if people fulfill their vows, will transform communities.

Membership exists to help us stay the course, to not give up when things get hard, and to be reminded in the wilderness of sin and doubt how to fix our eyes upon Jesus and his glory. Membership is not just an ideological position paper, delineating a set of theological pet peeves. Membership is a pledge to show up in each other's lives. To be there in real ways. And to make sacrifices for each other. In practical ways, it means that church membership in the visible church ought not to be broken lightly.

As a pastor's wife, I have seen the ugliest side of people when they start to believe that the sins of others in our church are intolerable, or when they pack up and leave instead of receiving the repentance of others, or sticking around long enough to work on reconciliation. The people who leave the church because they think they are too good for it have no idea the hurt that they cause—for the people who love them and miss them, and for the people hurt by the things they said and the things they didn't say when they broke fellowship.

Sin hurts the church. Public sins cause damage to the name of Christ and build horrific stumbling blocks between image bearers and their God. Sin brings down churches and families. But sometimes the smaller, private, socially acceptable sins can also be horrific. The sin of failing to reconcile because you think yourself better than your brothers or sisters can rot the life out of the fellowship of believers.

In my history in the church, I have witnessed the way both public and private sins destroy lives and relationships and render the covenant of church membership to be a matter of convenience, no more binding upon the conscience than your YMCA membership. This does irreparable harm to the witness of Christ. Public sins demand public repentance and/or public church discipline. A public sin has a known perpetrator and a known victim.

The church in Corinth had to deal with notorious public sins: thieves, drunks, adulterers, men who practiced homosexuality, and a man who lived openly and proudly in an incestuous relationship (and then later repented, broke off his relationship, and was restored into membership of the church). But the church in Corinth also had to deal with people who got drunk at the Lord's table, and people who used the church for their own ends and interests. God condemns both, and, with repentance and reconciliation, renews both kinds of sinner.

Importantly, church members are to be united in love, not shared social standing in the world of comparable lifestyle choices and interests. *The Westminster Confession of Faith* declares, "All saints...being united to one another in love...have communion in each other."[13] First John 4:10–12 declares, "In this is love, not that we loved God, but that He loved us and sent His Son to be the propitiation for our sins. Beloved, if God so loved us, we also ought to love one another. No one has seen God at any time; if we love one another, God abides in us, and His love is perfected in us." Because God is invisible, if our love for one another within the visible church is evident, God's love "is perfected" in us, or, completes us. We become useful vessels who reflect who God is. When he reconciled believers to himself, he also reconciled believers to one another.

The visible, local church is thus a community of believers united not in shared experiences or sociological categories or sin patterns, but in love. Diversity is necessary for real love for God and love for each other. One reason why it is hard for people to live in community is that we lack loyalty and we know it. We reason with ourselves that we will stick with a particular congregation until some precious line is crossed, and then we will pick up our church membership like so many marbles and take them elsewhere. With a church on every corner, we can afford infidelity, right? Loyalty to the church flies in the face of selfish ambition and self-love, as loyalty depends on personal sacrifice and the willingness to reconcile and forgive. Love for fellow believers should cause three things: loyalty within the local body of the church (and therefore resisting the temptations to break covenant vows for small offenses), opennness in confessing sin and seeking help for hidden shame, and fellowship with believers in other denominations.

Many sins work against this kind of love. One of the kindest things that church members can do is to check themselves against common sins that rip churches apart. These are, of course, big sins of adultery, murder, and abuse, deceptive living, hypocrisy, deceit. But they also include sins like gossip, anger, pride, and lack of forgiveness. Being a member of a church gives you daily practice at tending the graces of fidelity, respectability, hospitality, and peaceability. Failure to practice these graces leads believers who think more highly of themselves than others to take their marbles and find a church with "better" people. This may seem like a fair call. But there is a reason why people like this are called "well-intentioned dragons."[14] Disloyalty tears the church apart as easily as murder.

Every church split tells the unbelieving world that the church is a negligible artifact, a sentimental institutional relic at best, and not the triumph of Christ and his protection over the watching world. Every church split tells other believers that there is no real reason to join a church, suggesting that it is safer to just "rent" your seat until something that serves you better comes along.

Christian, if you trample on the church like this, when persecution comes, where will you go? When persecution comes, to where will you bring your neighbors?

Chesterton says that God makes your neighbors, even as you make your friends and your enemies. A similar principle can be extended to church membership: you don't choose your brothers and sisters in the church—God does. It is tempting to think that if only you could choose your brothers and sisters, all would be well. After all, doesn't it make sense that people who share the same hobbies and interests make for better brothers and sisters? Don't you want your children to be around people just like them—and you? Wouldn't you have more fun—and more friends—if the people in your church shared your peculiarities, sin patterns, and blind spots? Shouldn't you break your covenant vows to your church to widen your circle of friends? Not if you are a true believer. If you break the covenant of church membership because you don't like the people in your church, think about what you are doing. The Lord Jesus Christ died for the people you reject. You are trampling the blood of the Son of God under your feet.

The majestic hope for a world to which Jesus will return implies that the church is strong in love, doctrine, and community.

Christian community in the home, neighborhood, and from within the covenant of church membership leaves believers wide open for love and friendship. Effective ecumenical love roots in God's truth. And when this kind of love takes hold, chapter 7 of the book of Revelation gives us this word-picture as encouragement of what is inevitable:

> *9 After these things I looked, and behold, a great multitude which no one could count, from every nation and all tribes and peoples and tongues, standing before the throne and before the Lamb, clothed in white robes, and palm branches were in their hands;*
> *10 and they cry out with a loud voice, saying, "Salvation to our God who sits on the throne, and to the Lamb."*

Epilogue: Marriage, Ministry, Children

Life at the Butterfields' in Durham, N.C., 2015

Words are like table settings. They are washed and dried, cried over and polished, taken out of the cabinet, and put back in their place. These words from me on the pages of this book are themselves table settings. They express an invitation to come to the table, pour some coffee for yourself, and join me in my kitchen. Things have changed since the close of *Secret Thoughts*. Things have deepened since the close of *Secret Thoughts*.

We moved from Virginia to North Carolina in April 2012. That was a biggie. Next, the United States exploded with questions about marriage, rejections of biblical marriage, and introductions of gay marriage. That was a biggie, too. And because of God's transforming work in my life, there are questions from the fallout of my conversion, from the train wreck of it all—good questions, but hard ones—that I receive daily, and that I have had to face.

Fix your coffee any way you would like, and join me at the table.

Push the crumbs aside, and never mind Caspian, the orange tabby joining us on the table. He is a new guy here, a little skittish and quirky, but with a big purr.

I am grateful to God that his transforming forgiveness is also a teaching forgiveness, and a discipling journey. The Lord does not leave anyone stranded. So, I am grateful that my marriage to Kent deepens and becomes *more* as the years go by, and that it grows out of something that the Bible anticipates: married couples who are "equally yoked" grow together in faith and life, in union with Christ and union with each other, till death do us part. As Christians, Kent and I share a spiritual compatibility, and the Lord has faithfully matured, ripened, bloomed, and increased each of us through this.

I—like you—am asked constantly what my view of marriage is. It is the question on everyone's mind today. Of course, it is hard for me to come to this "what is marriage" question without hearing the speech-impaired minister (who never once pronounced the letter R correctly) in the movie *The Princess Bride* stumbling through a protracted verbal-marathon diatribe, oblivious to how his long-windedness is being used in the story line. And, the funny side of marriage is also a great gift from God. But jokes—in order to be funny—must rest on solid ground. A joke is something that we all know is not actually true. Because we have lost our sense of shared biblical knowledge about marriage, the joke is on us.

Many Christians cannot defend biblical marriage because we cannot define biblical marriage. I know that was the case for me. And unless we can define biblical marriage, we unwittingly become complicit with the problem, with God's image bearers reacting to the great tempestuous storm of our culture by stumbling around like the psalmist describes these men as doing in Psalm 107:27—"They reeled and staggered like a drunken man, and were at their wits' end." I believe today's culture storm is meant to lead people to do what the psalmist does in the line that follows: "then they cried to the Lord in their trouble, and He brought them out of their distresses" (Ps. 107:28).

Often these days, I am called to defend marriage: both my marriage and the institution of biblical marriage. After all, how can someone like me go through all of these permutations of affection? How could I have identified as heterosexual, lived for ten years with that identification, committed acts of sexual sin, come to despise it (the sex, not the sin)? How could I then develop sexual and affectional attractions to women, live in serially monogamous lesbian relationships for a decade, and, after coming to an understanding that the Bible is true and Jesus is risen, square off against my cavernous lust? And again, how could I have come to despise it (the sin, not the sex)? And then, how could I have married Kent after my train-wreck conversion? How could someone like me embrace this one-flesh union, seeing it as something that both transcends and transforms that messy bag of fallen desires that constitute personal feelings? How could I change? Did I change? What changed? How?

Some things are a mystery, and God's work in crafting his people is surely one of the greatest of mysteries. One thing that helped me understand my role in marriage was the reality that marriage is never only about two people. When Kent and I got married, we believed that we were better for the Lord together than separate. We wanted to be parents, and to raise children in a Christian home, with a praying mother and a praying father. While God did not open my womb, he opened my heart, and gave us children through adoption. It helped me to see and experience this, to see the enlarging and opening and developing and becoming that unfolds when God gives children to a covenant marriage.

Over the years of our marriage, Kent and I have grown closer as our family has grown up. We have grown through the problems and difficulties of mothering and fathering, some issues unique to people who, like us, adopted two teenagers out of foster care. It has always been vital that Kent and I stand together and are not divided by children, some of whom are skilled defense attorneys for parental manipulation. Our children, especially our older ones, brought boatloads of pain and betrayal with them. They needed to be both protected from harm and disciplined. This is a hard line to tow when you adopt people who start out a foot taller than you are. Growing in my role as a mother helped me to grow into my role as a wife. Growing in my role as a wife helped me to grow in my role as a mother. Using words like wife and mother are light years away from my old vocabulary of partner and parenting. I have come to understand that I am not (only) a parent. I am a mother. God taught me that I am not a partner, but a wife. Men and women have distinct roles and gifts, and I am slowly learning this. Like most of my most cherished life lessons, I am learning this quite late in life.

In a practical book entitled *What is Marriage? Man and Woman: A Defense*,[1] by Sherif Girgis, Ryan T. Anderson, and Robert P. George, the authors make the case that there is no such thing as parenting, arguing instead for mothering and fathering. When I first read this book (a week ago), many scattered loose ends came together for me. I must confess: I was more than a little hesitant to read this book. Books that rely on natural law tend to leave my stomach in knots. And because I read this book on a plane ride from Charlotte, N.C., to Tulsa, Okla., I did not want to endure a plane flight with a knotted stomach! But I was about to meet one of the authors and share a panel discussion at a conference, so reading the book was necessary and respectful to do. So I did it. I considered it my homework.

I read a lot of books for homework. But rarely has a book read for homework affected me like this. This book offered me the scholarly reprimand that I needed. I realized how my own vocabulary has been one of my holdouts for a worldview that still has invisible tendrils into my life.

So, here we are, at the close of this book. It's a sunny and crisp February day in Durham, N.C., where February sometimes means short sleeves and flip-flops. Just today, a crocus popped up in the patch of leaves and dirt that I see under the homeschool room window. I texted that picture to my friends in the North under the caption: "February in Durham." Just boasting in the Lord's goodness. Not rubbing it in. Not too much, that is.

Kent is pastoring the church that I mentioned at the end of *Secret Thoughts*. We are a small church committed to hospitality and outreach. Kent faithfully preaches the Word every Lord's Day, and we are always blessed when visitors join us for worship and the fellowship meal that follows the service. We gather weekly for a Wednesday night prayer meeting and twice a month for a women's book study. I teach our children's Sunday school class (on *Pilgrim's Progress*) with another mom and other helpers. In a small church, everybody matters. Everybody counts. You know and are known. We celebrate the Lord's Supper weekly, and the intensity and regularity of this sacrament brings union with Christ to the forefront of our worship each week. We sing psalms *a cappella* and I am one of three people who lead the congregation in singing. Nothing fancy. Kent loves serving God in this frontline way, and I love supporting him in this. We want to see our church grow in grace and numbers, and we covet your prayers for us.

Our teenage son is now a twenty-something fulltime fire fighter with his own apartment and life. Our adult daughter continues to live in another state and is happy at work. Our two little ones are old enough to make themselves mac and cheese when they don't like the lunch menu and to shoot a squirrel with a pellet gun. (NB: when you live in North Carolina, squirrel shooting is an art and science that crosses the line from sport to culture.) My mom, who lived with us for sixteen months until we drove her crazy, moved into a retirement community and lives about two miles away. Our beloved golden retriever, Sally, died unexpectedly of a fast-growing tumor last June, one month after we were robbed and she was beaten by the robbers. Always stalwart and sweet to the end, we miss her ninety-pound presence daily.

We continue to thrive in our homeschool. We live in a neighborhood with homeschool neighbors and resonant friends, who share with me the highs and ho-hums of school, ministry, health, and daily life. Neighborhood children who participate in homeschool together have become great, good friends, and the woods behind our house are filled now with hand-sawn forts — fruit of the labor of long days of building life together after piano practice and math are done.

Like all good conversations, this one that you and I share here will close for now. It is soon to be dinner time, and I will need to nag (uh, prompt) the children to set the table. Forks on the left, knives on the right. We will set a few extra plates. We have neighbors and church friends coming over, as usual. I put out two pots of soup on the stove this morning (blackeyed peas — southern style — and a vegetarian Indian lentil curry). I will cut the bread that I made yesterday and toss a salad. Friday is a soup and bread night — or pizza night — because our homeschool co-op meets at our home on Fridays and it is a day busy with Narnia novels and keyword outlines and kids forgetting to take their shoes off when they race through our house. Maybe after dinner and family devotions, we will watch a movie and I will get out my knitting. I'm making fingerless mittens for everyone this year, using some old mohair from my Syracuse yarn stash. These are good days. Full with meaning and paradox.

Life in the Lord is always a good mix of meaning and paradox.

I leave you with a favorite prayer poem that captures this, "Valley of Vision," from a book also called *The Valley of Vision*.[2]

Lord, high and holy, meek and lowly

Thou has brought me to the valley of vision,
where I live in the depths but see thee in the heights;
hemmed in by mountains of sin I behold thy glory.

Let me learn by paradox
that the way down is the way up,
that to be low is to be high,
that the broken heart is the healed heart,
that the contrite spirit is the rejoicing spirit,
that the repenting soul is the victorious soul,
that to have nothing is to possess all,
that to bear the cross is to wear the crown,
that to give is to receive,
that the valley is a place of vision.

Lord, in the daytime stars can be seen from the deepest wells,
and the deeper the wells the brighter thy stars shine;
Let me find thy light in my darkness,
thy life in my death,
thy joy in my sorrow,
thy grace in my sin,
thy riches in my poverty
thy glory in my valley.

Saints of old were often clear on a point on which contemporary Christians are muddled: you can't defend the right to yourself (including your right to pursue things that God has forbidden) and at the same time defend God's righteousness. We all are "hemmed in by mountains of sin." In the school of Christ, we will "learn by paradox" that to lose your life is to gain Christ. In Christ's strength, you must choose: you or God. If you choose yourself, you will always feel alone, even in a crowd or internet community of like-minded thinkers. This is because Christ knows you better than you do.

These are challenging times, to be sure, but these times are in God's sovereignty, too. And we are to thank God for these times, as he has providentially used them for our witness, allowing us to speak truth to our neighbors and friends who do not yet know the Lord. If we stand in Christ, we are not alone. If we stand in our own self-defense, we place ourselves in exile. But Jesus is living and he intercedes for us. Jesus promises. He promises to be "with [us] always, even to the end of the age" (Matt. 28:20).

In the Lord, each day holds the promises of God for you, with renewed mercies from the Lord to guide you as you face new challenges. Who knows what great things the Lord has for us today? With eyes to see and hands to help, open and unhindered by the Spirit through Christ's atoning love, imprinted on my heart by the gift of repentance. God alone knows the great things he crafts out of the details of our days.

Thank you, friend, for reading these thoughts. I pray that the Lord will anoint you as you pursue him. He is able to do immeasurably more than we ask or imagine, so pour out your heart to him. May he fill you with his truth, his salvation. May you walk in valor according to his calling for you, whether that calling takes you to grand or meager places. May you remember who you are, may you hold fast to Christ without wavering, may you contend for your faith, which is a precious jewel. May you test in the Word each little grace to see that it be sound and true. May our gracious Lord lead you into Christian friendships and family, church membership and community, so that you are strong in the family of God even when you are weak in yourself.

May you impact the world, extending the hand of our Savior to the lost and the lonely, the despised and the rejected. May you be clothed in the armor of God, and go to battle against sin and Satan with courage, holding nothing back. Together, may we see revival in this land as we go from God's strength to strength.

Amen. Peace be with you.

Acknowledgments

Now to Him who is able to keep you from stumbling, and to present you faultless before the presence of His glory with exceeding joy, To God our Savior, who alone is wise, be glory and majesty, dominion and power, both now and forever, Amen. (Jude 1:24)

For the past decade, I have heard my husband offer a benediction, the pastor's closing words which give praise to God, render thanksgiving for his steadfast love, and beg protection over those who bow before him. These words—and Kent's voice—have become a mosaic of memory for me, one that reminds me that the Rock of Christ will never disappoint, even—no, especially—when we are disappointed. Writing makes time stand still for me. Books make me face my fears. And morning after morning—I often write between 4 and 6 a.m.—as I worked on this book, I could hear Kent's voice behind God's Word, and that promise, that the Lord would keep me from stumbling. I cling to this promise. I cling every day to this promise.

At the writing of this book, I have been walking with Christ for sixteen years. My life now is full with the promises of God and the union with Christ that he promised. The looking back required by books like this is dangerous, disorienting, and frightening. After all, Lot's wife didn't become a memorial of looking in the wrong direction for nothing. Seductions lurk everywhere. Peering down into the details of my past—my life before Christ—is like hanging off of a cliff. In addition to Kent, the following people held my ankles as I dangled off the cliff of my past and tried to capture the inner landscape of my union with Christ. I thank you with all of my heart.

Thank you, Kent, my beloved husband, for shouldering and upholding me as I wrote this book and delivered many aspects of it in lectures, leaving you with a messy kitchen and messier still unfinished homeschool math homework.

Thank you, Knox and Mary, my beloved two youngest children, for giving up some of our precious time together so that I could close the door and write and get on airplanes and travel and speak.

Thank you, beloved Mom ("Grandma" to most everyone else), for sacrificing time with me so that I could write.

Thank you, beloved church family at First Reformed Presbyterian Church of Durham, for praying with me and for me as I faced this book. Special thanks to Debbie Leverett for using her superhuman organizational skills and getting my calendar and speaking schedule in order so that I could function. Thank you, Charlie Leverett, for helping me to get on my knees when I pray, for baking me a cake when I started to lose weight, and for leading our psalm sings with passion and care. Thank you also to my children's Sunday school buddy, Lauren Gonzalez, and to all of the children in our church. I pray that when I am an old lady one of you boys will someday be my pastor.

Thank you, beloved homeschool mom friends, for supporting me in prayer, meals, and childcare. Thank you for the joy of schooling our children together. Special thanks goes to Kara den Boef, Heather Mangum, Tonya Nelson, Hope Roberts, and Kristin Stults.

Thank you, beloved neighbors, for praying weekly with me and for helping me keep my perspective on the joy of neighboring: special love goes to Roy Averette, Bob and Donna Mutter, Andy and Tonya Nelson, Ryan and Kristin Stults, and Will and Hope Roberts.

Thank you, beloved staff at Crown & Covenant, for guiding and helping me write and think. Thank you, beloved editors,

Drew and Lynne Gordon, for quickly coming to my aid when the waves of doubt and the expectations of others overwhelmed me. Thank you for all of the behind-the-scenes details that you make right. Thank you, beloved staff: Danielle Pockras, Shelley Davis, Shelby Winkel, Becca Byers, Linda Au Parker, and artist Eileen Bechtold.

Thank you, beloved speaking and writing agents, who peered into the complex bio-system of my life and knew that I needed urgent help. Thank you for picking me up at airports, answering SOS text messages (usually from airports), and having solutions to my problems. Wes Yoder, thank you for being a man of grace who helps me whisper words of kindness even as the world shouts in hatred. Dana Ashley, thank you for knowing that I needed a Tiger Mama, and thank you for being so perfect in that role. Robert Wolgemuth, thank you for allowing me to know and love your precious Bobbie as she battled cancer and radiated Christ to her medical staff, finally winning the prize and beholding the Face of her Savior on October 28, 2014. Robert, you have encouraged me to think, write, and speak as a professional like no one else, and the Lord has used you to keep me afloat and to behold his sober call on my life as I sit alone at my desk in the dark of the morning.

Thank you, beloved sister and brother in Christ: Susanna Stevens, for traveling with me and reading every word I write, and for knowing how to make me laugh at myself; Christopher Yuan, for praying with me, for leading the way in this speaking ministry, for your courage, for your example of godliness.

Thank you, beloved Rebecca, for disagreeing with me and for giving me the chance to understand why. Thank you for your friendship; I know it is a risky one.

Thank you, beloved colleagues and friends, who have read portions of this manuscript or the whole enchilada and offered feedback that improved this book, sharpened me, softened me, and bettered me: Kent Butterfield, Denny Burk, Daniel Howe, Mark Jones, Michael Lefebvre, Robert Wolgemuth, Susanna Stevens, Barry York, Christopher Yuan, and Rebecca.

Notes

Preface

1 *Cassell's Latin Dictionary* (NY: Wiley Publishing, 1968), s.v. "redimo."

2 My thanks to Holly Stratten for first introducing this helpful distinction between facts and truth.

3 William Gurnall, *The Christian in Complete Armour (Edinburgh: Banner of Truth*, 1989), 15, quoted in Richard Rushing, ed., *Voices from the Past: Puritan Devotional Readings* (Edinburgh: Banner of Truth Trust, 2010), 16.

4 Sam Allberry, *Is God Anti-Gay? And Other Questions about Homosexuality, the Bible and Same-Sex Attraction* (Purcellville, VA: The Good Book Company, 2013), 77.

5 A revisionist hermeneutic is a reading practice that interprets Scripture through the "moral logic" of personal experience and social justice. See, for example,

James V. Brownson, *Bible, Gender, Sexuality: Reframing the Church's Debate on Same-Sex Relationships* (Grand Rapids: Eerdmans, 2013); and Matthew Vines, *God and the Gay Christian: The Biblical Case in Support of Same-Sex Relationships* (New York: Convergent Books, 2014).

6 See Judith Butler, *Gender Trouble: Feminism and the Subversion of Identity* (New York: Routledge, 1990); and Diana Fuss, *Essentially Speaking: Feminism, Nature, and Difference* (New York: Routledge, 1989).

7 If you have embraced this hermeneutic of separation, you have engaged in a *semi-Pelagiast* (believing that sin has not permeated our ability to reason and think) and *antinomian* (believing that the moral law of God is no longer binding) posture.

Chapter 1: Conversion

1   Lesbian sexuality seemed cleaner because its lack of penetration felt less violent to me. And because neither children could be conceived nor STDs transmitted (for the most part), I considered it unpolluted in comparison to heterosexual sex. I remember once being at a gay pride march and a self-identified Christian held up a placard that read: "AIDS is God's Curse on Homosexuals." A lesbian friend of mine quickly made up her own sign. It read: "If AIDS is God's Curse on Homosexuals, then Lesbians Must Be God's Chosen People." I suspect you get my drift here. In addition to sexual cleanliness, lesbianism seemed more moral because everything about it was based on egalitarianism.

2   Revelation 21:7, "He who overcomes will inherit these things, and I will be his God and he will be My son."

Chapter 2: Identity

1   Elias Pledger, in *Puritan Sermons 1659–1689* (Wheaton, IL: Richard Owen Roberts, 1981), 1:317–324, quoted in Rushing, ed., *Voices from the Past*, 157.

2   Richard B. Gaffin, Jr., translator's preface to *Adam in the New Testament: Mere Teaching Model or First Historical Man?* 2nd ed., by J.P. Versteeg (Phillipsburg, NJ: P&R, 2012), xiv.

3   Joel R. Beeke and Mark Jones, *A Puritan Theology: Doctrine for Life* (Grand Rapids: Reformation Heritage Books, 2012), 205.

4   "The Fall of Man," in *The Reformation Heritage KJV Study Bible*, ed. Joel Beeke (Grand Rapids: Reformation Heritage Books), 12.

5   Russell D. Moore, *Tempted and Tried: Temptation and the Triumph of Christ* (Wheaton, IL: Crossway, 2011), 18.

6   *The Works of John Owen* (Edinburgh: Banner of Truth, 1987), 3:469–471, quoted in Rushing, ed., *Voices from the Past*, 162.

7   The fact that one word may have more than one meaning, may change meanings over time, or may have a multiple set of complementary meanings, does not mean that we do not know what words mean. The difference between the sign (word) and the signifier (meaning) has long been understood as the root of poststructural reading and postmodern thinking. But, this linguistic theory makes for a poor excuse for failing to obey God.

8   John 15:3, "You are already clean because of the word which I have spoken to you," and John 17:17, "Sanctify them in the truth; Your word is truth."

9   Beeke and Jones, *A Puritan Theology*, 482.

10 Ephesians 2:5–7, "Even when we were dead in our transgressions, [God] made us alive together with Christ (by grace you have been saved), and raised us up with Him, and seated us with Him in the heavenly places in Christ Jesus, so that in the ages to come He might show the surpassing riches of His grace in kindness toward us in Christ Jesus." Theologians also use other words to describe this threefold union: 1) predestinarian, 2) redemptive-historical, and 3) existential. The words may differ, but the ideas are the same.

11 G. I. Williamson, *The Westminster Confession of Faith for Study Classes*, 2nd ed. (Phillipsburg, NJ: P&R, 2004), 58.

12 John Calvin, *Institutes of the Christian Religion*, ed. John T. McNeill, trans. Ford Lewis Battles (Philadelphia: Westminster, 1960), I.15.4.

13 Johannes G. Vos, *The Westminster Larger Catechism: A Commentary* (Phillipsburg, NJ: P&R, 2002), 167. See also 2 Cor. 3:18.

Chapter 3: Repentance

1 Jeff VanVonderen, *Tired of Trying to Measure Up* (Minneapolis, MN: Bethany House Publishers, 1989).

2 Jen Wilkin, "Failure Is Not a Virtue," *The Gospel Coalition* (blog), May 1, 2014, http://www.thegospelcoalition.org/article/failure-is-not-a-virtue.

3 VanVonderen, *Tired of Trying to Measure Up*, 128.

4 Noah Webster, *American Dictionary of the English Language* (1828; facsimile of the first edition, San Francisco: Foundation for American Christian Education, 2000), s.v. "admit."

5 Webster, *American Dictionary of the English Language*, s.v. "confess."

6 The Westminster Divines, *The Shorter Catechism with Scripture Proofs* (Edinburgh: Banner of Truth Trust, 1998), n.p. Originally published in 1648.

7 This is a gem of a book and a must-read. It begins with the nature of true repentance, and, as the adjective "true" might suggest, it also warns the reader about counterfeit repentance. Watson says that gospel repentance is "spiritual medicine made up of six special ingredients: 1) sight of sin; 2) sorrow for sin; 3) confession of sin; 4) shame for sin; 5) hatred for sin; 6) turning from sin" (18). Watson says that each ingredient is necessary for repentance to be true.

8 Beeke and Jones, *A Puritan Theology*, 4–5.

9 Ralph Venning, *Sin, the Plague of Plagues, or Sinful Sin the Worst of Evils* (London, 1669), 225–226, quoted in Beeke and Jones, *A Puritan Theology*, 203.

10 Alan Jacobs, *Original Sin: A Cultural History* (New York: Harper Collins, 2009), Kindle edition, introduction.

11 Jacobs, *Original Sin*, introduction.

12 Ibid.

13 Mary Shelley, *Frankenstein, or The Modern Prometheus*, the 1818 text, ed. James Rieger (Chicago: University of Chicago Press, 1982), 219.

14 One of the more intriguing facets of this book is the Creature's erudite reading list, including Milton's *Paradise Lost* and Goethe's *The Sorrows of Young Werther*.

15 Jacobs, *Original Sin*, introduction.

16 Beeke and Jones, *A Puritan Theology*, 208.

17 Anthony Burgess, *The Doctrine of Original Sin* (London, 1658), 89, quoted in Beeke and Jones, *A Puritan Theology*, 208.

18 *The Works of John Owen*, ed. William Goold (Edinburgh: Johnstone and Hunter [1850–1855]), 4:180, quoted in Beeke and Jones, *A Puritan Theology*, 210. Originally found in *Causes, Ways, and Means of Understanding the Mind of God* (1678).

19 *Overcoming Sin and Temptation: Three Classic Works by John Owen*, eds. Kelly Kapic and Justin Taylor (Wheaton, IL: Crossway, 2006), 51. Quote originally found in *On the Mortification of Sin in Believers* (1656).

20 Owen, *Overcoming Sin and Temptation*, 141. Originally found in *Of Temptation: The Nature and Power of It* (1658).

21 As this book goes into print, Mark Jones has written a new important book on Christology called *Knowing Christ*.

22 Mark Jones, *A Christian's Pocket Guide to Jesus Christ: An Introduction to Christology* (Fearn, Scotland: Christian Focus Publications, 2012), 25.

23 Donald Macleod, *The Person of Christ* (Downers Grove, IL: InterVarsity Press, 1998), 226. Quoted in Jones, *A Christian's Pocket Guide to Jesus Christ*, 28.

24 Psalm 22A, stanza 1 in *The Book of Psalms for Worship* (Pittsburgh: Crown & Covenant Publications, 2010).

25 Psalm 22E, stanza 14 in *The Book of Psalms for Worship*.

26 Russell D. Moore, *Tempted and Tried*, 21.

27 Quoted in Kris Lundgaard, *The Enemy Within: Straight Talk About the Power and Defeat of Sin* (Phillipsburg, NJ: P&R, 1998), 29.

28 *The Works of John Owen*, vol. 6, *Temptation and Sin*, 20, quoted in Rushing, ed., *Voices from the Past*, 55.

29 Because Owen's language may be off-putting to our modern ears, I recommend Kelly Kapic and Justin Taylor's edition, *Overcoming Sin and Temptation*, for its readability and references.

30 Kris Lundgaard, *The Enemy Within*, 39.

31 Owen, *Overcoming Sin and Temptation*, 133. Originally found in *On the Mortification of Sin in Believers* (1656).

32 Joshua 7:19, "Then Joshua said to Achan, 'My son, I implore you, give glory to the Lord, the God of Israel, and give praise to Him; and tell me now what you have done. Do not hide it from me.' "

33 Owen, *Overcoming Sin and Temptation*, 267. Originally found in *The Nature, Power, Deceit, and Prevalency of the Remainders of Indwelling Sin in Believers* (n.d.).

Chapter 4: Sexual Orientation

1 Nick Roen, "Same-Sex Attraction in Real Life," *Spiritual Friendship* (blog), February 12, 2015, spiritualfriendship. org/2015/02/12/same-sex-attraction-in-real-life/#more-4669.

2 Sigmund Freud, *The Future of an Illusion*, trans. and ed. James Strachey (New York: W.W. Norton, 1961), 43.

3 "Conventionally, the English Romantic period is defined by two kings, George III (1760–1821) and George IV (1821–1830); two wars, the American War of Independence (1775–1783) and the war against France (1789–1793); a political revolution in France (1789–1793), the Industrial Revolution in England (1780–1830), and so many cultural and scientific innovations that one observer, Lord Byron, called it 'the age of oddities.'" Marilyn Gaull, *English Romanticism: The Human Context* (New York: W.W. Norton, 1988), viii.

4 The study of the underlying principles that are present in all things and exist solely by virtue of their existence.

5 Michael W. Hannon, "Against Heterosexuality: The idea of sexual orientation is artificial and inhibits Christian witness," *First Things* (March 2014): 27–34.

6 Hannon, "Against Heterosexuality," 28.

7 Ibid., 30.

8 Ibid.

9 See, for example, Thabiti Anyabwile, "The Importance of Your Gag Reflex When Discussing Homosexuality and Gay Marriage," *The Gospel Coalition blog*, August 19, 2013, http://www. thegospelcoalition.org/blogs/

thabitianyabwile/2013/08/19/
the-importance-of-your-
gag-reflex-when-discussing-
homosexuality-and-gay-
marriage/

10 John Murray, *The Epistle to the Romans*, The New International Commentary on the New Testament (Grand Rapids: Eerdmans, 1959, repr. 1987), 47.

11 Hannon, "Against Heterosexuality," 30.

12 Creation ordinances are those commandments or jobs given to Adam and Eve before the fall: procreation, stewarding the earth, having dominion over the creatures, work, keeping the Sabbath holy, and marriage.

13 Vos, *The Westminster Larger Catechism*, 179.

14 Ibid., 202.

15 Ibid., 175.

16 Adrienne Rich, "Compulsory Heterosexuality and Lesbian existence." Originally published in 1980 and collected in *Blood, Bread, and Poetry: Selected Prose 1979–1985* (New York: W.W. Norton, 1986, reis. 1994).

17 Sexual essentialism is the belief that genitalia should determine sexual identity.

18 Rich, "Compulsory Heterosexuality," n.p.

19 Indeed, prior to reading the Bible for myself, I thought it

was drop-dead obvious that patriarchy was a sin. But after I read the Bible and after Christ claimed me for himself, I had to confront the fact that God held Adam accountable for eating the forbidden fruit. God held Adam accountable because Adam was Eve's (and my) federal head. This showed me that headship preceded the fall. Male headship, like everything else before the fall, was good.

Chapter 5: Self-Representation

1 Lesley Brown, ed., *The New Shorter Oxford English Dictionary on Historical Principles* (Oxford: Clarendon Press, 1993), s.v. "gay."

2 *Oxford English Dictionary*, s.v. "queer."

3 Andreas J. Köstenberger and Thomas R. Schreiner, eds. *Women in the Church: An Analysis and Application of 1 Timothy 2:9-15*, 2nd ed. (Grand Rapids: Baker Publishing Group, 1995, reis. 2005), 54.

4 Webster, *American Dictionary of the English Language*, s.v. "modify."

5 Norma W. Goldman, *English Grammar for Students of Latin*, 3rd ed. (Ann Arbor, MI: Olivia and Hill Press, 2007), 120.

6 1 Corinthians 1:13, "Has Christ been divided?"

7 Ephesians 4:22-24, "Lay aside the old self, which is being corrupted in accordance with the lusts of

deceit, and…be renewed in the spirit of your mind, and put on the new self, which in the likeness of God has been created in righteousness and holiness of the truth."

8 The following quotations are from Daniel Mattson's article, "Is 'Gay' Just Another Adjective?" *Crisis Magazine*, February 20, 2015. http://www.crisismagazine.com/2015/gay-just-another-adjective.

9 Raymond Williams, *Keywords: A Vocabulary of Culture and Society* (New York: Oxford University Press, 1983), 22.

10 Mark Yarhouse, *Understanding Sexual Identity: A Resource for Youth Ministry* (Grand Rapids: Zondervan, 2013), Kindle edition, endnotes.

11 Yarhouse, *Understanding Sexual Identity*, chap. 1.

12 Ibid.

13 Biblical feminist Rachel Held Evans has written a blog post on my conversion calling into question the problem of its "single story." See Rachel Held Evans, "Homosexuality, Evangelicalism, and the Danger of a Single Story," *Rachel Held Evans* (blog), November 4, 2013, http://rachelheldevans.com/blog/single-story-evangelicalism-homosexuality-butterfield-?rq=butterfield.

14 Yarhouse, *Understanding Sexual Identity*, chap. 1.

15 Yarhouse, *Understanding Sexual Identity*, chap. 6.

16 Ibid.

17 Those born with intersexuality have reproductive or sexual anatomy and/or chromosomes that do not fit typical expectations for a male or female.

18 Psalm 19:12-13, "Acquit me of hidden faults. Also, keep back Your servant from presumptuous [willful] sins; Let them not rule over me."

19 Williamson, *The Westminster Confession of Faith for Study Classes*, 234.

20 John Piper, MP3 format sound, April 29, 2007, http://www.desiringgod.org/sermons/single-in-christ-a-name-better-than-sons-and-daughters.

21 The Westminster Divines, *The Shorter Catechism with Scripture Proofs*, n.p.

22 Sam Allberry, *Is God Anti-Gay?*, 32.

23 Richard Baxter, *The Practical Works of Richard Baxter*, vol. 1, *A Christian Directory* (Morgan, PA: Soli Deo Gloria Publications, 2000), 78–79.

24 "Farewell Sermon," *The Works of Jonathan Edwards*, I:ccvi–ccvii, also quoted in Rushing, ed., *Voices from the Past*, page 7.

Chapter 6: Conflict

1 The interconnection of personal life with social activism.

2 An excellent introduction to Reparative Therapy can be found in Heath Lambert's article, "What's Wrong with Reparative Therapy?" *Association of Certified Biblical Counselors* (blog), November 17, 2014, http://www.biblicalcounseling. com/blog/what-wrong-with-reparative-therapy.

Chapter 7: Community

1 Russell D. Moore, *Adopted for Life: The Priority of Adoption for Christian Families & Churches* (Wheaton, IL: Crossway, 2009), 31.

2 The Westminster Divines, *The Shorter Catechism with Scripture Proofs*, 10.

3 Dietrich Bonhoeffer, *Life Together: A Discussion of Christian Fellowship*, trans. John W. Doberstein (NY: Harper & Row, 1954), 91.

4 Bonhoeffer, *Life Together*, 112.

5 We visit a local nursing home one Lord's Day each month, for a short worship service, followed by prayer and psalm singing.

6 Jay Pathak and Dave Runyon, *The Art of Neighboring: Building Genuine Relationships Right Outside Your Door* (Grand Rapids: Baker Books, 2012).

7 The following psalm selections may be found in *The Book of Psalms for Worship*, Psalm 23B.

8 Williamson, *The Westminster Confession of Faith for Study Classes*, 243.

9 Ibid.

10 Ibid., 244.

11 Ibid., 244.

12 Quoted in Philip Graham Ryken, ed., *The Communion of Saints: Living in Fellowship with the People of God* (Phillipsburg, NJ: P&R, 2001), 55.

13 Williamson, *The Westminster Confession of Faith for Study Classes*, 254.

14 Marshall Shelley, *Well-Intentioned Dragons: Ministering to Problem People in the Church* (Minneapolis, MN: Bethany House Publishers, 1994).

Epilogue

1 Sherif Girgis, Ryan T. Anderson, and Robert P. George, *What is Marriage? Man and Woman: A Defense* (New York: Encounter Books, 2012).

2 Arthur Bennet, ed., *The Valley of Vision: A Collection of Puritan Prayers and Devotions* (Edinburgh: Banner of Truth Press, 2011), xxiv–xxv.

Recommended Reading

Allberry, Sam. *Is God Anti-Gay? And Other Questions about Homosexuality, the Bible, and Same-Sex Attraction.* Purcellville, VA: The Good Book Co., 2013.

Baxter, Richard. *The Practical Works of Richard Baxter: Vol. 1, A Christian Directory.* 1846. Morgan, PA: Soli Deo Gloria Publications, 2000.

— — —. *The Saints Everlasting Rest.* 1856. ReadaClassic.com, 2012.

Beeke, Joel R. and Mark Jones, A *Puritan Theology: Doctrine for Life.* Grand Rapids: Reformation Heritage Books, 2012.

Bonhoeffer, Dietrich. *Life Together: A Discussion of Christian Fellowship.* Translated by John W. Doberstein. New York: Harper & Row, 1954.

Bridge, William. *A Lifting Up for the Downcast.* Banner of Truth Trust Puritan Paperback. 1649. Edinburgh: Banner of Truth Trust, 1995.

Brooks, Thomas. *Precious Remedies Against Satan's Devices.* Banner of Truth Trust Puritan Paperback. 1652. Edinburgh: Banner of Truth Trust, 1997.

Burk, Denny. *What is the Meaning of Sex?* Wheaton, IL: Crossway, 2013.

Burroughs, Jeremiah. *The Rare Jewel of Christian Contentment.* Banner of Truth Trust Puritan Paperback. 1648. Edinburgh: Banner of Truth Trust, 2002.

Bushell, Michael. *Songs of Zion: A Contemporary Case for Exclusive Psalmody.* Pittsburgh: Crown & Covenant Publications, 1999.

Calvin, John. *Institutes of the Christian Religion,* 2 vols. Edited by John T. McNeill. Translated by Ford Lewis Battles. The Library of Christian Classics. Philadelphia: Westminster Press, 1960.

deYoung, Kevin. *Taking God At His Words: Why the Bible Is Knowable, Necessary, and Enough, and What That Means for You and Me.* Wheaton, IL: Crossway, 2014.

———. *What Does the Bible Really Teach about Homosexuality?* Wheaton, IL: Crossway, 2015.

Freeman, John. *Hide or Seek: When Men Get Real with God about Sex.* Greensboro, NC: New Growth Press, 2014. (Also see harvestusa.org.)

Gagnon, Robert A. J. *The Bible and Homosexual Practice: Texts and Hermeneutics.* Nashville: Abingdon Press, 2001.

Girgis, Sherif, Ryan T. Anderson and Robert P. George. *What is Marriage? Man and Woman: A Defense.* New York: Encounter Books, 2012.

Goodwin, Thomas. *The Heart of Christ.* Banner of Truth Trust Puritan Paperbacks. 1651. Edinburgh: Banner of Truth Trust, 2011.

Hays, Richard B. *The Moral Vision of the New Testament: A Contemporary Introduction to New Testament Ethics.* San Francisco: Harper San Francisco, 1996.

Heyer, Walt. *Trading My Sorrows*, n.p.: Xulon Press, 2006. (Also see the author's website, sexchangeregret.com)

Horton, Michael. *Ordinary: Sustainable Faith in a Radical, Restless World.* Grand Rapids: Zondervan, 2014.

Jacobs, Alan. *Original Sin: A Cultural History.* Wheaton, IL: Crossway, 2001.

James, John Angell. *Female Piety: A Young Woman's Friend and Guide through Life to Immortality.* 1860. Morgan, PA: Soli Deo Gloria Publications, 1999.

Jones, Mark. *Antinomianism: Reformed Theology's Unwelcome Guest?* Phillipsburg, NJ: P&R, 2013.

———. *A Christian's Pocket Guide to Jesus Christ: An Introduction to Christology.* Fearn, Scotland: Christian Focus, 2012.

———. *Knowing Christ.* Edinburgh: Banner of Truth Trust, forthcoming.

Kapic, Kelly M. and Justin Taylor. *Overcoming Sin and Temptation: Three Classic Works by John Owen.* Wheaton, IL: Crossway, 2006.

Köstenberger, Andreas J. and Margaret Köstenberger. *God's Design for Man and Woman: A Biblical-Theological Survey.* Wheaton, IL: Crossway, 2014.

Kruger, Michael J. *Canon Revisited: Establishing the Origins and Authority of the New Testament Books.* Wheaton, IL: Crossway, 2012.

Lefebvre, Michael. *Singing the Songs of Jesus: Revisiting the Psalms.* Fearn, Scotland: Christian Focus, 2010.

Letham, Robert. *Union with Christ in Scripture, History, and Theology.* Phillipsburg, New Jersey: P&R, 2011.

Machen, J. Gresham. *Christianity and Liberalism.* Grand Rapids: Eerdmans, 1923.

Miller, C. John. *Repentance: A Daring Call to Real Surrender.* Ft. Washington, PA: CLC Publications, 2009.

Moore, Russell D. *Adopted for Life: The Priority of Adoption for Christian Families & Churches.* Wheaton, IL: Crossway, 2009.

— — —. *Tempted and Tried: Temptation and the Triumph of Christ.* Wheaton, IL: Crossway, 2011.

Murray, David. *Jesus on Every Page: 10 Simple Ways To Seek and Find Christ in the Old Testament.* Nashville: Thomas Nelson, 2013.

Murray, John. *The Epistle to the Romans,* 2 vols. Grand Rapids: Eerdmans, 1959, 1987.

Oliphant, K. Scott. *Covenantal Apologetics: Principles and Practice in Defense of Our Faith.* Wheaton, IL: Crossway, 2013.

Pink, Arthur. W. *Profiting from the Word.* Edinburgh: Banner of Truth Trust, 1970.

Pink, Arthur W. *Spiritual Union and Communion.* Collected in *Free Grace Broadcaster Issue 64: Union and Communion with Christ.* Also available on Kindle from Sovereign Grace Publishers.

Qureshi, Nabeel. *Seeking Allah, Finding Jesus: A Devout Muslim Encounters Christianity.* Grand Rapids: Zondervan, 2014.

Roberts, Maurice. *Union and Communion with Christ.* Grand Rapids: Reformation Heritage Books, 2008.

Rushing, Richard, ed. *Voices from the Past: Puritan Devotional Readings.* Edinburgh: Banner of Truth Press, 2009.

Rutherford, Samuel. *The Letters of Samuel Rutherford: A Selection.* 1664. Edinburgh: Banner of Truth Press, 2012.

Ryken, Philip Graham, ed. *The Communion of the Saints: Living in Fellowship with the People of God.* Phillipsburg, NJ: P&R, 2001.

Shaw, Ed. *The Plausibility Problem: The Church and Same-Sex Attraction.* Nottingham, UK: Intervarsity Press, 2015.

Sibbs, Richard. *The Bruised Reed.* Banner of Truth Puritan Paperback. 1630. Edinburgh: Banner of Truth Trust, 2005.

Stonehouse, N.B., and Paul Wooley, eds. *The Infallible Word: A Symposium by the Members of the Faculty of Westminster Theological Seminary.* 2nd ed. Phillipsburg, NJ: P&R, 2002.

Thomas, Derek. W. H. *How the Gospel Brings Us All the Way Home.* Lake Mary, FL: Reformation Trust Publishing, 2011.

Trueman, Carl R. *The Creedal Imperative.* Wheaton, IL: Crossway, 2012.

— — —. *The Real Scandal of the Evangelical Mind.* Chicago: Moody Publishers, 2011.

VanTil, Cornelius. *The Defense of the Faith.* Phillipsburg, NJ: P&R, 1955.

Venning, Ralph. *The Sinfulness of Sin.* Banner of Truth Trust Puritan Paperback. 1669. Edinburgh: Banner of Truth Press, 1993.

Versteeg, J.P. *Adam in the New Testament: Mere Teaching Model or First Historical Man?* Translated by Richard B. Gaffin. Phillipsburg, NJ: P&R, 2012.

Vos, Geerhardus. *Biblical Theology: Old and New Testaments.* 1948. Edinburgh: Banner of Truth Press, 1996.

Vos, Johannes G. *The Westminster Larger Catechism: A Commentary.* Edited by G. I. Williamson. Phillipsburg, NJ: P&R, 2002.

Wall, J. K. *Messiah the Prince Revisited.* Pittsburgh: Crown & Covenant Publications, 2014.

Warfield, Benjamin Breckinridge. *The Inspiration and Authority of the Bible.* Phillipsburg, NJ: P&R, 1948.

Watson, Thomas. *The Doctrine of Repentance.* 1668. Edinburgh: Banner of Truth Trust, 1999.

— — —. *The Ten Commandments.* 1692. Edinburgh: Banner of Truth Trust, 2009.

Wells, David F. *No Place for Truth: Or, Whatever Happened to Evangelical Theology?* Grand Rapids: Eerdmans, 1994.

Williamson, G. I., ed. *The Westminster Confession of Faith for Study Classes.* Phillipsburg, NJ: P&R, 2004.

Yuan, Christopher, and Yuan, Angela. *Out of a Far Country: A Gay Son's Journey to God. A Broken Mother's Search for Hope.* Colorado Springs, CO: WaterBrook, 2011.

For more information about this author, visit

www.rosariabutterfield.com

Other Titles from Crown & Covenant Publications

Secret Thoughts of an Unlikely Convert
Expanded Edition
Rosaria Butterfield

The Gospel & Sexual Orientation

Messiah the Prince
William Symington

Messiah the Prince Revisited
J. K. Wall

Presbyterian & Reformed Life Series
Sing the Lord's Song
Faith of Our Fathers
Joyful Voices
Biblical Baptism
Christ's Covenant and Your Life